"'Isn't the mind amazi͟ᵧ ͟ ͟ ͟ ͟ ͣͪ͟ᵧ ͭͪᵢₙᵧ is possible?'
asks author Tina Tau in her masterful dream-inspired
memoir. This captivating book will make readers feel that
they can live a different life if only they pay attention to
dreams, the inherent unruliness of the soul, the natural
wildness of the heart, and the unpredictable trajectory of
the spirit."

—Victoria Rabinowe, artist, author, director
of DreamingArts Studio, Santa Fe

"Tina Tau's memoir shows us how to turn mess into magic.
She tells her transformative tale with an incandescent blend
of humility and healing, wildness and wonder. "

—Raphael Cushnir, author of *Surfing Your Inner Sea*

"*Ask for Horses* is an initiation into the alchemies of wonder.
As we accompany this speaker on her epic, dream-guided
journey of discovery, her dance with destiny becomes our
own. We enter a chorus of deep wisdom. We are illuminated
by poetic grace. We are awakened by awe. We are called
home to our own deep soul knowing."

—Sage Cohen, author of *Fierce on the Page*

"When you enter this book, prepare to grow luminous,
to travel in company with someone offering 'jewels of
information' about electric connections between dreams
and actions. Prepare to recognize how the liquid bounty of
the inner life may offer guidance for the thirsty tangle of the
outer life."

—Kim Stafford, author of *Singer Come from Afar*

Ask for Horses

MEMOIR OF A DREAM-GUIDED LIFE

Tina Tau

Kelson Books
Portland, Oregon

Published by KELSON BOOKS
2033 SE Lincoln, Portland, Oregon 97214
kelsonbooks@gmail.com

Cover image: Matrioshka/Shutterstock
Design: Steve Connell Book Design | *steveconnell.net*

Kelson Books are printed on paper from certified sustainable
forestry practices.

Printed in the United States of America.

ISBN 978-0-9827838-8-7

Library of Congress Control Number: 2022937645

The unconscious element of our being from which the dreams spring is so much older, wiser, stronger, more creative, loving and reconciling than we even imagine...
— Jeremy Taylor

The Soul that rises with us, our life's Star,
Hath had elsewhere its setting,
And cometh from afar:
Not in entire forgetfulness,
And not in utter nakedness,
But trailing clouds of glory do we come.

— William Wordsworth

Live to the point of tears.
— Albert Camus

CONTENTS

(Dreams in italics)

INTRODUCTION

I grew up hearing Quakers talk about "that of God" in everyone. I always pictured that piece of God as a little spark of
divinity inside us—like a gold ring in a cherry pie. Something
glowing, of a different nature, hidden and small. But my
dreams have taught me to see this differently. "That of God"
in us has more motion, more urgency, than a ring. It is not
finished. It is something like the tree inside an acorn—"the
force that through the green fuse drives the flower," in Dylan
Thomas's words. It is potent, like an underground aquifer, or
a snowstorm, or Mozart's Requiem, or the look in a red-tailed
hawk's eye. It's both fiercely impersonal and fiercely personal.
It has the power, and the intent, to make us more alive. It wants
us to join with it, to ride the wingedness of it, and it will use
any glint of light, or avalanche, or field of bluebells, or intense
dream to shake us out of our dullness and sense of separation.
This wild intelligence—life itself—arises from both within and
outside me, in some way that seems stranger the longer I live
with it. And one of the ways it makes itself known in my life is
in my dreams.

I've chronicled hundreds of dreams over the course of my
lifetime but only forty of them appear in this book. These
are dreams that struck me deeply at the time I had them and
that still reverberate. They revealed things about myself that I
didn't want to see. They tried to awaken me, to nudge or shove
me toward wholeness. And, as you will see, they very much

9

wanted me to write this book.

One thing struck me as I wrote: how untethered dreams are to time as we know it. A few of the dreams in this book knew what was going to happen long before I did—sometimes in crazy detail. They planted answers years or months before my waking self even asked the questions. They knew, for instance, when the baby was conceived who I would later adopt, and what kind of person she would be. They saw a bad breakup coming long before I did, and how I would heal from it. Some dreams are not decodable in the moment, because the moment they are written for has not come yet. But if you carry them around with you and wonder about them, when their moment arrives you will likely feel a shiver.

Dear reader, I hope that shiver of awareness, when a dream suddenly makes sense to you, becomes part of your life. That shiver is the leading edge of wonder. And wonder has the power to pry open, to crack open, our shell of alienation. Our dreams arise from an ancient, inherent source. The Earth, you might say, is dreaming us. If we pay attention to the dreams she sends, we might start to accept that this is where we belong. We might remember we are animals. We might sprout wings and whiskers, might start to live on our planet as if we loved it here.

An eerie, gorgeous picture gleams through this narrative, I hope—of a numinous world, blazing with intelligence and generosity, the wellspring from which our dreams appear. The world in which the hawk glides, who sees the whole snow-capped landscape of my life, and who floats, watching, as I stumble and skip along the trail.

One more thing—a word about how this book is organized.

The basic pattern is Story-from-waking-life; Dream; Reflection on the dream. Often there's a fourth bit, which you might call "Tina-now," where I zoom out and comment or provide a frame for the first three parts. There are lots of variations, but these are the basic pieces of the pattern.

Also, another voice—Hawkeye—speaks up now and then. I will just let that voice speak for itself.

ONE

In which I am surprised

CANCER

September 2021
68 years old

> *The eternal makes you urgent.*
> —John O'Donahue

In a PET scan, your body is flooded with radioactive dye. It pools in places with a lot of activity—your brain, for instance, or cancer tumors. Cross-section images of your body are taken as you ride slowly on a narrow bed through a white machine. It all takes about an hour and a half. A couple of hours later you can sit in a doctor's office and look inside your—my!—body.

My doctor wears glasses, a face mask, and a scratched, smudged face shield. Her bright eyes shine through all of that. She scrolls down the scan on her computer screen, starting at the top of my head, with my all-lit-up brain. Your brain is always active, so a PET scan isn't reliable for tumors there; you have to get an MRI for that.

Mostly my scan looks dark on her screen, with white blobs for bones. She points out spinal cord, ribs, as she slides down through my chest. We're looking for places with a purple glow. Here's some: a little arthritis in the spine.

Ah. Here's what we're really hunting: a bright purple tumor in my left lung. Another in the right lung. And here—glowing white, splendid, powerful, well beyond purple—is the original tumor, in the base of my left lung.

"Here's where it probably started. Probably years ago. You've never smoked?" she says.

"No."

"It doesn't seem to be anywhere else in your body. The MRI found no sign of it in your brain. Lung cancer is sneaky," she says, "it likes to sneak around into the brain, but this hasn't."

"This is not curable—" she looks me in the eye—"but it *is* treatable."

"We've analyzed the fluid that came out of your lung. This cancer has certain genetic markers that allow it to be treated with a targeted treatment, a daily pill that is much less harsh than standard chemo. You'll keep your hair; it won't suppress your immune system."

Sitting in this windowless office looking at scans of my beautiful body, holding my partner Steve's hand, I'm hurting. Yesterday I got out of the hospital, after a surgeon put a catheter in my lung. It will allow me to drain lung fluid at home, a good thing. But my back hurts from the surgery, and my mind is hot with overload. I swallow an oxycodone. It will make me dizzy in a few minutes. But I think, I hope, we're at the end of this visit. I'm grateful the doctor is wise. I'm relieved that I'm not facing the poison hammer of chemo. But so much has happened so fast, I don't even know how else I'm feeling. I'm surfing a firehose of information, with no wits to spare for processing.

Ten days ago I stopped in at urgent care on a sunny September morning, between errands. I felt fine—buoyant, cheerful—but I was getting breathless climbing hills. I thought maybe I had an infection and would get some antibiotics, could swing by Costco and be home for lunch.

Instead, the high-voltage electrical sizzle of change. The doctor—with her long gray braid and tattooed arms—holds my hand. I tell her my younger sisters died from cancer ten years ago. I tell her, "Since they died, I have tried to stay far away from the medical-industrial complex." She gets it, I can see. I cry. We look together at the chest x-ray, which shows my left lung completely occluded: full of liquid, not air. She packs me off to the ER. "I've called them, they're expecting you."

At the ER they drain a quart of fluid out of my left lung. It hurts like hell. I go through MRI and CT scans—all new to me. A doctor comes by with a small fleet of residents. I cry again when they tell me I haven't done anything wrong. I'm admitted to the hospital. I stay two nights. I have a hard time wrapping my mind around the word "cancer."

I know it's true—but what does it mean?

PREPARING FOR THE BIG ONE – *Dream*

August 20, 2021
67 years old

A big storm is coming, a hurricane. I'm on the ground floor of a two-story house with another woman. The power goes out. It comes back on in a little while. Then a flash flood rushes through the house, three or four feet of water, but it recedes as well. I realize this is the front edge of the storm, and *we've been warned.*

It isn't my house, and I don't know where the candles are kept, but now we have time to find them. We'll move up to the second floor to be out of the flooding. We can also make some calls before the cell service goes down. My friend is making the calls, asking people how widespread the storm is, while I fill a washtub in the yard with clean water. A small, dried-up pig is stuck to the bottom of the washtub and I'm pulling on it to get it unstuck. It wouldn't be the worst thing to have it in the clean water but it would be better if it were out of there.

This dream came three weeks before I went to urgent care, before the firehose nozzle turned to On.

I thought that it must be a warning about something coming for Steve, who has complicated health issues. I thought it was saying that it was time to get ourselves ready for some bad news, a big health storm. To marshal our inner forces. To collect candles — our sources of warmth and light, our friends, and our spiritual resources. I wondered about that little dried up pig, though. No sense of what that might be.

The overall spirit of the dream was such a sharp sense of warning — the Big One is on the way and we have a little time to prepare.

I was right about the warning. I just didn't know whose body the storm was going to appear in.

Now, two months into my treatment, I see another level of the dream. The symbolic minutes we were given to prepare were not so much the three weeks between the dream and the diagnosis, as the space I'm in right now, when the treatment is working and I feel pretty good. A window of time to get ready for the storm of my actual dying, when the power will really go out.

The little pig in the washtub: could that be a tumor in my lung? — something that doesn't belong in there, that I am trying to dislodge? If so, what a non-scary, almost funny image of it!

WHAT WAS THAT ABOUT?

All of this makes a person look back at her life and think about things. Things like—what was *that* about? That life I've just lived—did I give it my best shot?

I've always been a person who wonders. I've known there was a bigger reality at the edge of what I could see, ever since I was four years old, playing in a branch of the great New England forest downhill from our house. It smelled of leaf mold and water, and it took me in with room to spare, like a stone falling into a pool. The same earth magic that pushed the pink lady-slipper orchids up out of the duff and populated the stream with orange salamanders ran through me. I didn't need words to know that I was alive and part of it. I'm still being tugged by that sense of mystery and looking for portals, for daily glimpses of that wider, stranger reality.

I sit this afternoon in my old low red armchair. All around me are bookshelves and books. Books I've bound, books from my childhood, books full of poems, art, *Pogo* cartoons, fairy tales, and Shakespeare. When I moved in with Steve I gave away half my books—about a thousand. The ones here, survivors of many culls, are precious witnesses and old friends. Leather-bound with gilded spines, tattered and split, glossy, big as a platter, small enough to hide in a pocket.

My feet rest on a blue rug my mother made sixty years ago. I watched her tear the long soft strips of wool and braid them, making a quiet place in the room as she worked. The rug itself makes a quiet place in this room. A good place to reflect.

I have Stage IV lung cancer. I have had it for years, without a clue.

What else haven't I noticed?

And how do I find out what I don't know?

With a pen. Or a laptop. There's one more precious book in this room—the one on my lap, coming out of my fingers, the one you are reading. It's well past time to finish it. I don't want to die without holding a copy in my hands. I want it to be a doorway, a window, into that wider, stranger reality. For this to happen, I have to keep my hands on the keyboard. Truth be told, I am a student of this book, even more than its author. As I work on it, it works on me.

It asks me to choose a lens for looking back over my life. What kind of story was it? A hero's journey, a saga of survival, a still-unsolved mystery?

It asks me to come out of hiding.

To be more honest with myself than I like. Am I brave enough to say what I've learned?

Time is short! It always was, but I feel it now. I hope I have a few more years. The drug—Osimertinib—is already shrinking the cancer, yay, and I'll take it as long as it works. But the tumors figure out how to get around it eventually. Right now I'm tired, and sometimes queasy, but mostly amazed.

HAWKEYE

We're right here, honey.
You know us now, far better than you did
when you set out to run away from yourself
50 years ago.

All we ask is that you let us love you.
Let's hear you tell
your beautiful story.

TWO
In which I begin to run

HAWKEYE

We were with you before Norma and Jim met
at the little Quaker college in Ohio.
Before the Mexican women stroked Norma's round belly
in the Veracruz sunlight, so happy for her.
Our hands caught you when you entered the air of Earth.
We will be there to catch you
when you breathe out your last breath.

THE MOON MAN — *Nightmare*

Portland, Oregon
1967
14 years old

It's night. I'm standing in a tower with deep-red walls and high arched openings all around. I'm looking out at the stars, at peace.

Suddenly I realize that the Moon Man is coming up the stairs. I panic. I run down the stairs and pass him as he is climbing up. He doesn't seem to notice me. He has a round, pale human face, wears a business suit, and looks tired.

I get to the bottom of the stairs. It is sunny. I keep running—not sprinting, but pacing myself for the long haul. I stop to drink water, to chat with some people; it all looks normal, but I know I will be on the run for the rest of my life.

I wake with my heart racing, knowing the Moon Man is coming up. I lie in the dark, stiff and terrified, for hours. The house is still.

My parents' bedroom underneath mine is quiet.

My father and mother are good people. My mom is loving and anxious, my dad musical and funny. With four kids already underfoot, my dad quit teaching junior high school, got a doctorate from Harvard, and became a Reed College professor. I admire the heck out of him. But I don't think he knows me. I'm quiet and thin-skinned, and he is glib, quick. He doesn't wait to hear what I want to say. Also, I am afraid of his temper. He rarely but harshly gets mad at us: cutting and sharp as an underwater reef. Some place wild and small, three years old and soft as an oyster, froze inside me when he yelled and I was little. It has never thawed. I just keep that tender part hidden.

But I've never heard him yell at my mom. Until now.

So when their voices start stabbing up through the floorboards—even my gentle mother is shouting!—I lie there cold. No one says anything in the morning. My fear has nowhere to go. I shove it down into that well-hidden place with my secret heart. My parents' marriage is liquidizing. How can it be? I thought they were solid. My *family*.

What the night-time yelling does to my younger sisters, Barbara and Kathryn, or my brother, Richard, sleeping—or listening—in rooms down the hall, I have no idea. No one says a word.

I am fourteen, just softening into a woman.

This dream shows how dangerous this threshold moment feels.

I stand, as I embark on womanhood, in a magical, sexual, feminine space—a dark red tower, open to the stars. But when I know this space is being penetrated, I can't bear it. No one should come here. The very thought of it is terror. I abandon my sexual center, which opens to the universe.

And once I'm down the stairs, I'm away. I don't even know whether the Moon Man is chasing me. He might be waiting in the tower. I don't care. I'm gone.

At fourteen, lying there stiff and sweaty, expecting the Moon Man's footstep on the stairs, I have no idea that this nightmare means anything. But looking back, I'm amazed at how well it predicts some odd things about my life. First, that I will move more or less constantly—an average of once a year—until I'm forty. Often thousands of miles at a time. And second, that I won't be able to build a solid relationship. Partly, of course, because I move every few minutes.

But not only that. When I pass the Moon Man on the stairs, he doesn't *see* me. This fits with my belief that my dad doesn't really know me, a belief that will turn out to be key to my nutty love life: I ache to be seen, but don't expect it to happen.

That yelling below my floorboards? My dad was having an affair with a graduate student. More than one, as it happens. It is 1968, after all.

I go to a Quaker boarding school in Canada for the last two years of high school. While I am away, they get a divorce (though neither of them calls to tell me this—my mom asks the principal of my school to tell me). My mother buys her own place, an old Portland house with roses painted on the living room ceiling. She gets a masters in teaching ESL and starts teaching Hmong and Mien refugees. When I come home for Christmas or summer vacation I look at my mom and am impressed. She loves her work, treasures her students. I wonder, uneasily—was that marriage a cage for both of them?

My dad moves into a big communal house in Northwest Portland. I like having dinner over there, playing Authors with his quick-witted housemates—teachers and filmmakers. I don't *think* I'm mad at my dad; there's a lively freedom in him that I didn't feel before, and I like it.

But on some bone-marrow level, oh dear, it's a different story. My mother's unspoken wound (and my own, even less admissible) stays frozen in me, black as basalt. I refuse to think about it, but I know that my mom was hurt. And below the radar, I blame my dad.

I tell myself that *I* will, by God, do it differently. When I finally get married I will be so committed you can steer a boat by my light. I'll make up for how my dad did it. No matter what hard stuff I have to wade through, I'll be all in.

That hard intention, mixed with skittishness, becomes a crazy relationship cocktail. There are moments over the next few decades when love fills my sails. But not for long. I don't know how to sit with pain, or talk to anyone about it, and I don't ask myself what I really want. I am not at home: I have abdicated my place and my power, left that calm red tower.

As I study this dream from here, decades later, I am touched by its accurate prediction of another thing about my life: It will look normal to other people, and will *feel* normal to me. It won't seem like a nightmare. It will look sunny and fine. There's nothing obviously wrong with me: I'm affectionate, curious, have nice thick hair. The panic stays underground, unseen—while I run and run, pretending everything is okay.

As a little kid, I loved a book called *The Golden Book of Poetry*. One of the poems in there, "Moon Song" by Mildred Plew Meigs, features the Moon Man.

> *And the waves roll out and the waves roll in*
> *And the nodding night wind blows*
> *But why the moon man fishes the sea*
> *Only the moon man knows.*

In the full-page illustration accompanying this poem, the Moon Man is a benevolent golden face, looking down on little mermaids playing at the edge of the sea. He is fatherly. It should be a comforting scene, but it isn't: my wariness about my dad let me cast the Moon Man as a villain. And of course there is the sexual layer to the story. The Moon Man belongs to the night, to what is unknown, to the mystery. He fishes, croons, cuddles!—but what he fishes for, no one knows. Yikes. That's super unsafe territory. This nightmare is a story in which I say no—not to sex *per se*—but to the possibility of trusting anyone with my body enough to go into the dark with them, to a place I cannot control.

MY FIRST TASTE OF DREAMWORK

Argenta, British Columbia
1970

I'm seventeen years old, short and strong and thin, with round glasses and dark curly un-brushed hair. I stand next to my friend Mary, her woodstove warming the backs of our legs. I'm telling her a dream. Deep snow and December dark outside the cabin make the reds and greens in the braided rug glow a little brighter, and the small room feels snug.

The miner's cabin she shares with her boyfriend is tucked back into the woods across the road from the two main buildings of Argenta Friends School: the Quaker Meetinghouse and the old hotel.

The hotel is a relic of the silver mine boom in the 1890s. Picture a rickety two-story rooming house in a Western movie, the kind you could pull down with a rope and a strong dog. You couldn't pull the Meetinghouse down, though, with any number of dogs. A dozen yards downhill from the hotel across a sloping lawn, it is new, handmade, and beautiful, made of golden peeled logs, with windows onto the shining north end of a ninety-mile-long, one-mile-wide lake.

If you came to sit in this Meetinghouse in silence every morning for two years, you might get to know the reflection of Meadow Mountain in that mile of Kootenay Lake water pretty well. You might feel guarded by the steady, wakeful presence of glacial mountains marching south down both sides of the lake, east into the Purcells, west into the Selkirks, north into the Rockies—endless slopes of granite, ice, scree, silence, moss, Doug fir, and hemlock, webbed by a few roads, a dam or two, narrow lakes, icy streams, black bears, the odd human. If you climbed one of those ridges, you would see nothing but snowy ranges all the way to heaven, or Banff. Sitting day after day in the presence of those peaks, you might feel safe.

My first visit to Argenta, three years ago, was a thunderclap of joy: I arrived in the dark after a bumpy ride in the back of the mail truck from Nelson. When I came out in the morning onto the grass between the hotel and the Meetinghouse, there it all was. The *mountains*. The lake, clear as dawn. Kids who looked like me, with long hair and work clothes, lying on the lawn. White-blossomed apple trees. The log Meetinghouse, with its triangular blue outhouse. I inhaled the clean high air, the space. It was balm to some place in me I didn't even know was sore. I smelled woodsmoke and lake water and wet grass and apple blossoms.

This is a school?

The silver miners who named Argenta —which until a few years ago had to be reached by ferry— are long gone. Only about a hundred people live here now. It would be easy to pass through this hamlet and not realize you'd seen it—just a few cabins scattered for about two miles along a narrow dirt road. The ferry dock is the thing to look for. And a hand-painted sign on the road above the dock: ENTERING ARGENTA: ARE YOU LOST, OR CRAZY?

The spread-out cabins hold loggers and farmers (who feel neither lost nor crazy, and don't care for the sign), and draft dodgers, and back-to-the-landers like Rob and Mary. Also a few dozen Quakers, who'd arrived in the early fifties: hardy families who believed Canada would be a better place to raise their kids than McCarthy-grim America.

Modern Quakers come in two flavors, "church" and "silent meeting." By and large (though not always) this means "conservative" and "liberal." Neither branch much resembles the passionate rebels of the seventeenth century. Nor do we wear the plain clothes that used to distinguish us—like the black hat on the Quaker Oats guy. About half the Quakers in the world are Africans (the church Quakers have missions and missionaries), but in the US both branches consist mostly of earnest white people.

The Quakers who moved to Argenta in the fifties belong to the same silent-meeting, social justice, simple-living branch of Quakerism that I grew up in. In 1960 they started a tiny school—Argenta Friends School. It was mainly a school for their own children, but a few Quaker kids from the States and Canada enrolled every year as well. All told there are never more than twenty-four students. We are more of a kin group, a tribe, than a school.

I knit myself into this tribe as surely as my friends knit socks during classes. People are few and precious out here at the end of the road; settlements like Argenta are freckles on the face of the folded, endless forest. There is no store for miles. Nowhere to spend money. No televisions. No streetlights. We generate our own electricity from Argenta Creek, tumbling icy down from Mount Willet. We live, cook, chop wood, dig gardens as part of staff families. We all sit every morning in the mountain-fed silence for half an hour, becoming more precious to each other. I feel lucky lucky lucky to be a student here.

So here I am, in Mary and Rob's cabin, telling Mary a dream. She is a few years older than me, with bright dark eyes and bouncy almost-black hair.

MUD – *Dream*

1970
17 years old

My sisters and brother and I come to a stream that we have to
jump across. I'm leading, and because I'm going first I don't
quite make it. I land in the mud on the other side of the stream.

Mary smiles at me. She's already understood it.

"Oh, well, Tina. Your parents are getting a divorce, right?"

The fire crackles. My heart sinks. I nod.

"So, in this dream, you have to cross a creek with your sisters and brother. Being oldest, you have to jump first. That seems like it could mean a couple of things. You have to leave the nest first. But also you have to find your way across the change that this divorce makes in your family—you have to lead the way across that."

Tears are starting to spring in my eyes.

"And it's so hard to go first that you end up in the mud on the other side. You are paying some kind of hard price for being the oldest child."

A lurch of recognition, compounded with delight and awe, hits my gut. How did the dream do that? How did Mary do that? It is a sensation of both flame and hunger, this discovery that dreams speak in a code that can be cracked—a code that, when cracked, leaves me with jewels of information.

A METHOD OF REFLECTION

Many years later, I will study with the Jungian, social-justice oriented dream teacher Jeremy Taylor. One thing I learn from him is how important that feeling is, the click I had when Mary talked about my dream. That "aha!," the delighted recognition, like getting a joke or solving a puzzle—that sensation is the key to understanding any dream. That's how you know you're on the track of what it wants to say.

Jeremy gave me some big, beautiful tools for dreamwork—starting with certain assumptions about the unconscious intelligence that creates our dreams. That intelligence, he says, is always trying to bring us into greater wholeness. All dreams, even nightmares, he says, come in the service of healing. He handed me two more, rather surprising assumptions: Dreams never come to tell us what we already know. And—we don't dream of problems we can't do anything about.

He showed me how even a tiny fragment can be important; sometimes that scrap of a dream is like a poem distilled from the prose of the night's dreaming.

He was always firm on the notion that only the dreamer knows what the dream means—with that "aha" as the compass—so when you give someone input on their dream, be aware that you are only and always projecting. The respectful language for this is, "If this were my dream . . ." or "In my imagined version of your dream . . ."

More will be revealed later about how Jeremy works, and especially about how dreams can serve as a force for social change, but it's good to know this much as we get started.

BREATHING MEMORIES

Argenta, British Columbia
1971
17 years old

I stop in the dark on the dirt road. The mountain stars glitter overhead; the lake lies still and immense beyond the trees. I look up for a second at the stars, and a wave of sweetness ripples through my body like mild electricity. It is a grateful shudder of well-being, as if light or energy is stirring through all my limbs: a rush of sheer aliveness I've never felt before. The clean smell of fir and tamarack, the packed dirt of the road, the coolness off the lake rises through me.

I know the road underfoot by feel. I like walking it in the dark. My sense that Argenta is *where I am meant to be* deepens with each ramble up and down that road at night. It is the spring of my senior year at the Friends School, and I am as happy as an apple tree in bloom. I live in one of the scruffy upstairs rooms of the old hotel with my roommate, Polly, a sassy long-legged poet.

In March, stretched thin from happiness and hard work, I get a cold.

After a few days of lying in bed blowing my nose, I wake with an unlikely sensation in my breath, or my mind—as rich as that moment of well-being on the dirt road, and maybe linked to it, but subtler, stranger, continuous. It's in the realm of experience where words don't travel well. The best I can do is say that a window has opened inside me, and a sweeter, cleaner wind from *somewhere else* blows in. It is almost, but not quite, a smell. Or more like a memory—memory is closer than smell. A memory of something wonderful, but I have no idea what it is. It is so nourishing. Pleasant beyond my ability to say.

It has a distinct, tender, glacial or tree-sap flavor, not in any way the tenor of my ordinary thoughts, which keep going along as usual. It is most present in the mornings when I first wake up but lasts faintly all day. It lingers about two weeks, a clear spring of wonder at the rim of my awareness, while I recover from my cold, write papers, romp with my draft dodger boyfriend, Terry, in his converted chicken coop up the road, chop any amount of wood.

As my cold gets better, the sensation fades. But then I get another cold, and the wonderful thing turns back on. I end up with a cold for the entire spring of my senior year, about three months. I don't know what this visitation is, truly, but I suspect that the cold keeps renewing itself on purpose so that this haunting sweetness will last. I don't tell anyone about it, being afraid to chase it away, but in my mind I call it "breathing memories."

And this same spring I have a bright series of dreams.

DEEP ALASKA — *Recurring Dream*

Argenta, British Columbia
1971

I visit a place called Deep Alaska. It is blue and gold, with immense hillsides lit from within. The hillsides are blue, with gold light over and inside them, and sometimes the hillsides are gold, with intense blue sky. There are no details to this landscape, no trees or edges; it is all color and light.

I realize that every place in our world corresponds to a place in another realm which has this deeper quality, a glow or force to it. There is a town in this blue and gold world called Great Hastings, which corresponds to a town called Hastings in our world. I don't see the town, I only hear about it. The word "Great" seems to mean the same as "Deep"—a more luminous version of the regular world.

The "breathing memories," *Deep Alaska* dreams, and the rush of well-being on the starlit road were, I think, facets of a single flowering—an unbidden, untrained awakening with its roots in physical joy. That spring of 1971 was strange and strong enough to reverberate, in various ways, for the rest of my life.

A couple of forces were at work to bring this about. For one thing, I was wildly at home in my animal body. I walked miles up and down the dirt road, had lots of playful (if not open-hearted) sex with Terry, did yoga before dawn in the Meetinghouse, raced barefoot through snow from the sauna to the black-cold lake. And I was happy, in a way I'd never been before and have seldom been since—the happiness of deep belonging.

As the burners of my body and heart turned on, they burned through something, some blockage in me, and the cold somehow turned a key, giving me access to a bigger—and quite other—world. The wind that gave me the beyond-normal-happiness haunting stream of "memories" blew straight down off those gold and blue dream hillsides. I was granted, for a couple of months, a chance to visit the place where I belong. Not just to Argenta, which cracked the window open, but to a vaster, luminous place within.

And then the school year ends. Graduation from the Friends School, for my class of eight students, is held in a high meadow with goats and dogs and crowns of flowers. Green-gray Mount Willet and Meadow Mountain stand watch. It is a cascade of love.

My friends go home. I'm not a student anymore; my parents are fully distracted by their divorce. No one talks to me about college. Since I don't know what to do, and can't bear to leave Argenta, I move into the chicken coop with Terry. The breathing memories vanish. Terry and I get a goat, for milk. She howls for her herd and after a few weeks we give her back.

KIM

Portland, Oregon
Summer 1972
18 years old

Terry's tiny cabin by Argenta Creek is too small for every part
of me. I haul mountain water in buckets out of the stream, grind
wheat berries to make bread like bricks, make stew from a bear
Terry shot. But I'm lonely for my friends who graduated, went
to college, went home. Snow swirls through the fir trees and I
watch it, wondering what to do. Howling silently for my herd.

By January I have it: I will go to Norway and learn
Norwegian, and then find the village that my great-grandfather
Omen Tow sailed from when he was eighteen. I'll travel in
England and Ireland. I'll set foot on the ground of my ances-
tors, recent and distant.

I leave Terry and the snowdrifts and the winter stars and go
back to Oregon. I stay with my mother in her rose-ceilinged
house, and work as a nanny for two sets of twins, saving up for
the trip. Portland begins to bloom and green, and in May I go
to a party.

Pat, a Reed College student I'd met folk dancing, is as slight
as a wren and as deep and unexpected as a red-rock canyon.
She has a little gathering one evening at her apartment, and I
bring gingerbread. Dense, perfect, molasses-y. Her tall friend
Kim, with a big nose and keen eyes, stands at the table telling her about his senior art show for the Museum Art School.
"Rainbows and shadows," he says. He eats a piece of gingerbread, and looks intently at me for a moment. A tiny wondering frown. And then looks away.

On my own, one afternoon, I visit the student show at the
Art Museum. His work stands out, but of course I would think
so. A papier-mâché rainbow as big as a loveseat, suspended
from the ceiling, unfolds and opens like a flower at the top.
Another rainbow comes out of the wall. With a projector you

can create your own shadows. I wander through his sculptures, feeling the quiet snowflakes of the intangible.

I know a book this man will like.

I buy big sheets of heavy cream paper and a good black pen and sit for many evenings at a table in my mother's living room copying out *The Golden Key*, an old book by George MacDonald. Two children, Tangle and Mossy, find and lose each other in a wilderness of shadows as they search for the golden key which opens the rainbow.

It is a translucent fable, about 130 pages—a long book to copy out. But because it is my own strange form of courtship, it is thrilling. My hair might as well be made of tungsten, blazing away as I sit there copying. When it's done, I make a blue paper cover, sew it down the middle, put it in a plastic bag, and bury it in the woods.

I make a treasure hunt through the city with clues hidden in my favorite places—the children's bookstore in Old Town, a floating dock set into the riverwall, the book *Ondine* in a locked cabinet at the library, a grove of trees by Lovejoy Fountain.

And he actually does it—follows the clues and digs up the book. "Once I figured out how your mind worked," he tells me, amused.

He cried when he finished the book, he said.

We go for walks in the city summer streets, smelling roses and exhaust. We lie on the flat roof of his downtown apartment, holding hands, watching night fall through the lattice of a dome he'd built up there. At his sunny small table he reads to me from "The Evening Song of Senlin" by Conrad Aiken:

It is moonlight. Alone in the silence
I ascend my stairs once more,
While waves, remote in a pale blue starlight,
Crash on a white sand shore.

We kiss, dance, visit Pat, talk of mountains and adventures, read poetry, make breakfast in his tiny kitchen. His apartment is like the rest of him—wonderful and odd. His vases are old green cathode ray TV tubes. He views the world through a different, brilliant, pane of glass.

We both know I am leaving in the fall. He approves.

"One of the things I like about you," he says, "is that you do what you say you're going to do. Lots of people say they're going to Europe, but they're just talking. You're really going."

I am. But I feel a kind of panic as the summer winds down. The attention of this gentle, angular man has ignited me. Everything seems more fragrant, more possible, more sacred in the presence of his sideways intelligence. It is hard to believe I am leaving. For a *year*.

What are we to each other? I never ask, we never say. He gives me some cards of an illuminated Book of Hours to take with me, and I leave him with a book about Everest. It tears a ragged hole in me to get in the car with the two women who give me a ride to New Hampshire in late September.

***

Near the end of *The Golden Key*, Tangle (having wandered for years) arrives at the cave of the Old Man of the Earth:

> *Then the Old Man of the Earth stooped over the floor of the cave, raised a huge stone from it, and left it leaning. It disclosed a great hole that went plumb-down.*
> *"That is the way," he said.*
> *"But there are no stairs."*
> *"You must throw yourself in. There is no other way."*
> —George MacDonald

I have thrown myself in. Down, down, plumb-down, through a few months of rainbow. And then shadow.

What this leap into love costs me, and what it gives me, is a tale that will take me years to tell, as we shall see.

MY YEAR OF EUROPEAN WANDERING

1972–73
19 years old

The Pan Am flight from Boston to Copenhagen gets in late. I shiver as I walk out of the airport wearing my green Kelty pack embroidered with my name: *Tina Wallace*. Distant lights; windy sea-smelling air. I have an open plane ticket good for a year, $800 in traveler's checks, and a Danish dictionary. Confused, tired, and mindful of having to make $800 last all year, I find a park bench near a hedge and unroll my sleeping bag underneath it. The next day I go into the city and catch a bus. For hours we drive past brown flat winter fields. The driver lets me off on a country road near Vejen and I walk to the school, whose square modern tower is visible from the bus stop. I've paid for a six-month term at Askov Folkehøskole, and here I am. I'm nineteen years old, and the wind is cold.

Askov, a school specializing in folk crafts, was my Danish uncle Bent's idea. I wanted to go to Norway. But Bent said no. "The Norwegian folk schools are religious. You wouldn't like it. You should go to Askov, it is more cosmopolitan. They have a class in Danish for Foreigners. Danish is similar to Norwegian, it will work just fine for you in Norway."

What did I know? He was the only person helping me. So here I am.

I take classes in filmmaking, embroidery, life drawing, music appreciation, pottery—whatever I can learn without talking. The food is a revelation: it tastes like it's straight from the farm, and probably it is. I have a cozy, dark-walled dorm room, which I decorate with the Book of Hours cards that Kim gave me.

But I don't feel good. I am uneasy in this flat, wind-scoured landscape. It is the opposite of Argenta. Not a mountain to be seen. The tallest point in the whole country is 170 meters. And I am such a stranger. I tell my classmates not to talk to me in English, because I am determined to learn their language, which is a good idea but makes me as dumb as a stone teapot. My main friend, Susan—the other American—is a mean, smart, wealthy girl. She gives me a book by Doris Lessing, *The Four-Gated City*, which alters my view of the world, but she also teaches me to shoplift. This makes the Quaker in me cringe. Worst of all, I miss Kim and am afraid I have lost him by leaving on my trip. I try to warm up by sleeping with any man who will have me.

On the other hand, two great things happen. After about three months of feeling like a preschooler, I start to speak and dream in Danish.

And I learn to bind books.

The school owns a building about a mile away from the campus that began its life as a windmill. The tall tower with the canvas sails burned, maybe a century ago, and now—strange and wonderful—the dome of a small astronomical observatory sits there instead, on the round metal track that used to turn the sails into the wind.

The bookbindery is a narrow room below the observatory, full of wooden presses, cupboards of paper and goatskin and knives. I fall into that room like a leaf onto a river. My teacher even gives me a key so I can go and work at night. Some nights I climb the wooden stairs and run my hands along the heavy brass telescopes, potent and glimmering. My love of stars and of old books is stirred together here with a mysterious big spoon. And the repurposing of the mill as an observatory delights me, though it will be years before I understand that I crave to be transformed in that same way.

In May, when the sun comes back to Denmark, I hitchhike to England with my friend Sylvia, who was one of my classmates in Argenta and has just finished hotel school in Switzerland.

Once, we run into trouble. A long-haul truck driver in Holland tries to get Sylvia into his bunk at the back of the cab. We fend him off and finally, resentfully, he lets us out on a busy freeway in the middle of the night. This fiasco lands us in Amsterdam after midnight with nowhere to stay.

We are saved by something we did earlier that day. When a car had stopped for us, we gave the ride to a tall, wild-haired Dutch boy who was having trouble getting a lift. He yelled an address out the window as the car drove off.

Since we didn't plan to stop in Amsterdam, we just waved back—but somehow we remembered the address. Thus, at pitch-dark two in the morning, we knock on a tall wooden door in Prinsenstraat. That curly haired young man and his friend are still up. Expecting us! We sag with relief and sleep on their floor. It feels like one of those old stories where the hero shares his bread and cheese with a beggar—a beggar who turns out to be King of the Fairies and saves the hero's life.

Sylvia and I press on to Belgium and a ferry across the Channel. When I step off the ferry in Dover I'm suddenly elated—a liquid, flowering, earth-warm, lark-ascending happiness.

As the bus for London cruises north through the emerald quiltwork of fields, I stare out the window, swelling with joy. Of course this is partly relief at hearing English again. But it feels like coming home. One layer of this feeling, one green patch in the quilt, is the sweet wind blowing off the Hundred Acre Wood, and the hush of rushes along Mole and Ratty's river—the quiet magical landscape of my childhood books. But there's more to this haunting sensation: a sense of familiarity, longing, of countless lives planted here, history flowing through hedgerows and under bridges; of my own lives laid down like leaves melting into the duff of the woods.

In London I find a tall, easygoing boy to stay with. His roommates mutter about freeloaders, but I don't stay long. I take myself over to the Council for British Archaeology on one of London's tiny back streets and land a summer job in Cornwall as an archaeological digger.

Off I go to the sea-lit green, tangled southwest tip of England. I join a small crew of about fifteen diggers. We work for an archaeologist named Henrietta. Most of the other diggers work for her every summer. We earn a few pounds, enough to buy food and beer, and we live together in an old stone farmhouse outside St. Austell. Dropping into this world gives me a kind of cozy, ancient thrill. I love the high green hedges filled with fuchsia, the hunt through layers of dirt for evidence of long-ago lives, and sitting around the farmhouse courtyard tired after work, listening and laughing. I'm back inside myself. Sunlight. The bright rippling face of the sea. Working with my hands. It's good.

Our first dig is a Bronze Age gravesite from 3,000 years ago, on a hill with a view of the blue Atlantic. We locate the grave—everything melted away by now—and a maze of quartz pebbles laid out around it. After a month we bring our trowels down to sea level and unearth the round huts and fire-pits of a small edge-of-the-world settlement from around 400 CE when the Romans still occupied Britain. Tin from Cornwall was traded all over the Mediterranean then. This site, Trethurgy Round, is surprising enough, interesting enough, to make the TV news. It's amazing to see it emerge under our hands.

The summer ends, the wind picks up, and I put out my thumb. I go to Wales and Ireland and Scotland, sometimes alone, sometimes with my red-rock-canyon friend Pat, who has come to London to get a doctorate in ancient Irish calligraphy. I climb the highest ridges I can find: Corran Tuathail in Ireland, Ben Lomond in Scotland. I seek out heartbreaking music in Irish pubs, visit friends from the dig in a hidden Welsh valley and a tiny Scottish island. I stand astonished in the chamber of Newgrange, under the tons of corbelled stone.

Everywhere, people are good to me, driving out of their way to the youth hostel or the trailhead or some local treasure they think I should see. Pat and I get lost one evening in North Wales looking for the cottage where my friend from the dig lives, and we knock on a farmhouse door. Two women, round and delighted, leave their ironing and run laughing down the road to show us the well-hidden path.

In October, as the days darken, I catch a ship from England

to the west coast of Norway. A ferry from Stavanger takes me to the village of Tau—the home of my great-grandpa Omen Knudsen, renamed Omen Tow when he reached America—where I am taken in by my grandmother's elderly cousins. She sent them food during WWII, and they sent back red and white mittens, which I wore as a child. These two old people treat me like a daughter. They have no English, but my Danish works fine, as uncle Bent said it would. I am so exhausted. In the warmth of their gentle welcome, as I let myself relax, I get a wicked, stay-in-bed cold.

The steep Norwegian mountains and long bright fjords turn on the same burners as Argenta. The breathing memories, which have been asleep for two years, kick back on. In Tau, at last, I've come to the place I've been looking for through my year of European wandering: troll-haunted, ancestral, glacial. The miraculous sense of breathing in a "wind from elsewhere" lasts a couple of silvery weeks, as I get better from my cold, leave my old cousins and hitchhike south to Kristiansand. There I catch the ferry back to Denmark.

The breathing memories vanish the day I get back to Denmark, where I'll catch my flight home from Copenhagen. Pretty, tame, flat Denmark just doesn't do it for me, in the way that wild Norway does. It's like when I graduated from Argenta Friends School: as I subtly constrict, the beautiful faint feelings or memories go away.

I've circled the North Sea, and it is time to go home. I've been on the road too long, with too little money. A year to the day from my arrival in Copenhagen, I fly back to Boston.

I have two quarters in my pocket—my entire fortune—when we land. It's enough to call my aunt and uncle in New Hampshire from a pay phone at Logan Airport. They drive down and pick me up, stop at McDonald's and get me some food, take me back to Wolfeboro, and let me rest for a week. I am translucent with weariness. My parents send me a ticket back to Portland, where my mother has made me a welcome-home pie. I feel like a bird falling out of the sky, caught by the kind hands of family: my old Norwegian cousins, my aunt and uncle in New Hampshire, my parents. I am grateful, and broken-winged.

✧✧✧

Kim and I talk one night as we stand outside the Reed Student Union during a break between folk dances. He gathers that I am hanging onto something that he has let go of.

"It wasn't what you thought," he says. "You made our relationship into something it wasn't." The soulful wail of a goatskin bagpipe in a Bulgarian dance tune floods out the door and pools around my feet like dark water.

PONDERING MY ADVENTURE

On that journey through Europe, that long hard year—what was I?

Not a tourist. Too wild and broke for that. Not a pilgrim, though that's closer—I had no holy destination, unless you count Tau. At times a wanderer, letting the wind take me to the next high ridge. I think the word is *seeker*. I was a magic-seeking creature. By magic I mean wilderness, deep history, secret doorways, echoes, tangled hedgerows, powerful weather, lilting and smoking fiddle tunes, standing stones, old libraries.

I knew about my quest for liminality (not that I knew the word), but I was also on a darker quest that I didn't know about. I was pushing past the edges of the good girl I was raised to be, to see what happened. Something in me needed to know where my own boundaries were. But that was a tough assignment, requiring being far from home, unguarded and lonely, for a good long chunk of time. It scared me, and it scarred me. The trip as a whole was a test I maybe, barely, passed.

That year of travel had great gifts in it: bookbinding, archaeology, Irish music, Norwegian mountains—but I was more unprotected, more exposed, day after day, than I have ever been. Sleeping under benches. Shoplifting. Picking up guys in laundromats. What was I thinking?

For one thing, I thought I was alone . . .

But I was not. I was helped over and over by people along the way.

If this adventure were a dream, the message would be that *kindness is water*: the source of life.

You can't live without it. *And* it is everywhere.

Strangers were so nice to me.

When I was hitching rides, drivers went out of their way to take me where I wanted to go. A busy family in England brought me home for Sunday dinner. People fed me, walked with me, told me about themselves. My old relatives in Norway gave me shelter after a hard year; my aunt and uncle salvaged me from the airport in Boston; my parents sent me a ticket home.

Being exposed, needing help, let me see how generous most people are. It let me feel their caring. It let me see the love that runs over the grass like a clear sheet of water.

How to make sense of all this sleeping around? It seemed normal at the time, and harmless, as long as I didn't get pregnant. In the late sixties, the rules had been cancelled. Birth control was easy to get. The whole pot of cultural norms was thrown into the air and fell down around us, messy as mashed potatoes. My father, who in another era might have guarded me, was caught in the same downpour, having affairs. My mother was swamped, trying to rebuild her life.

My parents were so absent at this time that I concluded, at sixteen, that I was a grownup. One sunny afternoon on the old ferry dock in Argenta, I felt a sense of agency, of adulthood, fall over me like a mantle. It was time, I realized, to be done blaming my parents or counting on them; my boat was now mine to steer. It was a brave, bright feeling. But that good feeling perched on top of a molten layer of denial, grief, arrogance, and vulnerability—and I had no idea.

Normal for the times or no, all that sex wasn't harmless. It started off all right. Playing with Terry in his chicken coop was potent, animal fun, and part of my unfolding awakening. I was fond of him—but not in love. It got worse from there. For the next several years, I was adrift. When I felt lovable I didn't seek sexual comfort, and when I felt alone, ashamed, scared, I did. I never slept with Kim, for instance, because I truly loved him. In Denmark, stumbling over the language, lonely, and cold, I didn't care who warmed me up. It was a way to be held. Then when I got to the dig in Cornwall, and had good friends and work I liked, I was content to nest in my sleeping bag alone.

This was odd. Why have sex with people I didn't care about, but not with those I did? The Moon Man dream is helpful here: the driving force behind this behavior was terror. My fear of being invaded in my most intimate place—that star-lit burgundy tower—led me to abandon it and go on the run. From the time of that dream, I was divided. For some years, I managed to have sex only by emotionally shutting down.

It's as if I was an electrical wire that could only carry so much current; on some level I believed I would overheat if I tried to run the heavy currents of love and sex at the same time. If I allowed myself to be caught—to love someone, to need them, to surrender to them—it would be too much, I'd be in mortal danger. Of what? Being left—being hurt—being rejected? I did not trust that a man would love me. That's the infected root of the panic.

I did real harm. I cost my partners the possibility of real connection, at the very least. But I hurt myself, too, in at least two serious ways. First, I injured my soft inner parts. Either the IUD I got while I was in Denmark, or some STD like chlamydia, left scars on my uterus and fallopian tubes that would cause a lot of trouble later.

And I felt so guilty. I knew I had to stop but had no gentle way of doing it. For the rest of my twenties and then through two misguided marriages, I pulled on myself with a harsh rein, trying to slow down. I thought I could force myself to be faithful, to be good. I was determined not to be that wild and unreliable person anymore. But a harsh rein is not good for the horses of the soul. That will cost me as well.

HAWKEYE

Oh, honey, you've thrown yourself in.
There is, as the Old Man of the Earth told you,
no other way.

You belong here. *Trailing clouds of glory*
and your own wildwood childhood,
you crave the touch
of this world. Dancing barefoot in the snow.
Gleaning magic from toast and fog and alpenglow.
The Earth loves you.
The smoke and moss of it
salvage you. This love is sap in your veins,
a lamp for your path.

And if anyone needs a lamp,
it's you, dear heart. Running headlong in the dark,
slipping on cave-stones.
You don't know what chases you
and will not stop to learn.

Our wings are under you.

THREE

In which I hear a voice

WHALES AND TUMBLEWEED

Southern Oregon: Gold Hill, Medford, Ashland
1973–1976
20–23 years old

After Europe, I move around (of course). I work as a dish-washer, a gardener, a bookstore clerk, a bookbinder, a carpenter and logger, and end up as a teacher in a small farm school. I don't go to college: how would I pay for that?

At the farm school, I learn to milk the Jersey cow. I'm good at it and love it. Leaning my sleepy head on the wall of her warm flank, smelling hay and milk and old barn, I enjoy the rhythmic squeeze, the zing of the milk squirting into the bucket.

I also learn to drive because I'm living in the country and there are no buses. But just as strongly as I am pro-cow, I am anti-car. This makes it hard to learn to drive. I blast through a stop sign in front of a cop on my first day out. I barely pass my driver's test on the third time I try.

The school is tiny (eight 7th graders, one of them my darling sister Kathryn). It's run by the parents of my good friend Cindy, who had been my first roommate in Argenta. Cindy's quiet, blue-eyed, brown-bearded brother Ted works on the farm and eventually ends up in my bed in my small cabin near the barn. Our first night together, I wake with a dream of a nest of kittens sleeping on my belly: a pile of warmth and comfort. He is gentle and intelligent and very shy. But he takes me into the back country, which opens my heart right up.

We drive to Scammon's Lagoon in Baja California, Mexico, where the gray whales come to calve. The water is so salty that no calf can sink! From our campsite on the sand we board a little boat, and out on the lagoon I reach out and stroke the barnacled, gritty back of a huge whale.

We camp at the edge of Klamath Lake and watch white-winged pelicans sail overhead in the blue twilight, big and quiet as angels. We hike in the Trinity Alps and the Kalmiopsis Wilderness, where the breath of the Earth is clean and ancient and awake. Walking those soft duff trails, I am lifted, rising into the wordless presence of the great trees. We ski into a remote hot spring in Idaho and lie in the hot water, snowflakes cold and light on our faces, our bodies barely submerged.

He also gives me my one and only technical climb: Mount Thielsen, near Crater Lake. We rise before dawn and set off in the snow from our base camp, Ted carrying the heavy coil of rope and all the know-how. Several hours later, we rope up for the last sheer bit of the climb. At the peak we watch the sun spread over the bright, waking-up Earth. I feel the insane joy of standing on a spire of rock at the top of the world, exhilaration in every ragged breath. Then we glissade down the mountain on pieces of cardboard, ice axes grabbing now and again at the crunchy snow to slow our careening slide.

Those wonder-laden trips into the feathered, snowy, salty, old-growth life of the world unfold my soul. They thrill me, and I love being out with Ted in the wild places. But I am still a nutbar. Restless, tumultuous, hungry. Wordlessly aching about the loss of Kim, confused about my dad.

An amazing bit of healing does happen with my father during the year I live at the farm. One afternoon, I'm driving on the freeway with my dad and his new girlfriend in his car. I have a meeting in Salem, a meeting of Quaker activists. I'm still learning to drive and a menace on the public roads. I swerve in the wrong place, and my dad yells at me—for the first time in years. I get out of the car sick and shaking, and have to leave my meeting after ten minutes and go into a side room and cry. I weep for two hours with my friend Bear holding my hand. As I sob I realize how disconnected from my dad I have felt since I was a very little girl. I write him a letter telling him this, and he writes back, a miraculous letter of apology. It's so tender. I feel like the clean world after a thunderstorm.

But then, shit, he goes and marries that new girlfriend, a drippy woman his own age. They get married at the farm school. The only thing I like about the wedding is making the wedding cake: I invent a recipe that uses only things we grow on the farm. Walnuts, wheat, eggs, cream, and honey. They ask me to speak at the service, but I have nothing to say. I am in full unconscious freakout. Affairs with graduate students is one thing; marrying a pale and sappy imitation of my mother is another. Why break up the family in the first place, then? I leave Ted and fly north, ending up on a dry, hot Indian reservation in central British Columbia. I use my rage to cut down trees for log fences. I drive a tractor snarling and crunching through the woods. A chainsaw is exactly the tool for my pain. I call it logging, but it is rampage.

Ted drives two thousand miles and finds me on my tractor, in my woe.

"I didn't think you were really done with me," he says. It is brave and kind of him to know this, and to drive so far to tell me. My heart softens, and I come back to southern Oregon to live with him.

We rent an old farmhouse in the pear orchards near Medford, with his two friends, Sam and John. The guys make exquisite hardwood looms, and I start a tiny bookbinding business called Snowbound Books. Chickens scratch around the melons and tomatoes in the overgrown garden. We write poems and songs. I try to be lovable, and loving. But truly, I am not able. Part of me is a ball of thorns, a slippery fish, a river on fire. I need someone to talk to. I need a counselor, though I have no money for one, and so after a year or so I finally give up on dear, quiet Ted and take up with a teacher of co-counseling.

Paul is a fair-haired Quaker, a champion fencer, a brilliant listener. He is my lover, but also my teacher. He holds my hands all night one night to keep me from doing something stupid, and in the morning I am on fire with life; no one has ever cared enough to do that before. He teaches me co-counseling. We stay together for a year, living in different cities but seeing each other often. I start to relax. I feel known. I release hours of tears. But when he mentions one day that I am not the woman

of his dreams, I break off with him, crack, like a stick snapping.
This startles him; he hadn't meant to chase me away.

"You're just scared!" he says.

"No, I'm not."

Oh, honey.

❋❋❋

In my first drafts of this book, I left this whole brouhaha—Ted
and our numinous treks into the wildwood, the healing with
my dad that bloomed from two hours of crying, my summer
as a logger for the Alkali Lake Tribe, my inchoate need for a
counselor which drove me to take up with Paul—all of that—
out of this story. Given that these years were such a crucible
time, so rich and hard, why on earth leave them out?

Well, there was no dream to attach these years to, except
those kittens on my belly on my first night with Ted. But the
real reason is that I was cringing; that time is still a little hot to
the touch. Part of me sharply judges the girl who left Ted. He
was the right man for a healthy version of me. I broke his heart,
as Kim broke mine, and I'm sorry.

As I turn the lenses in my hand, wondering what lens to
look through when I cast my eye back over my life, I decide
to put it all back in. How can I fail to mention that I touched a
mama whale, or stood aglow on the peak of Mount Thielsen?
Or that I was, for a while, a tumbleweed with a chainsaw?

Another part of me that I strangely failed to mention in earlier drafts is the young Quaker activist. All the while I am living in southern Oregon, binding books, milking cows, and being jittery about love, I'm doing political organizing. I even appear on TV.

So here comes a question that has dogged me all my life: how does effective change happen? How do we confront the monstrous, heavy ship of capitalism and economic inequality, militarism and deep-sea mining, extinctions and waste and clear-cuts? How do we lean steadily enough and in the right place to prevent an utter crash?

Where, against that ship, is the point of most leverage?

At twenty-one I take on the Department of Defense. They are hosting a week-long series of courses, lectures, movies for military officers and the public at Southern Oregon College, called a "National Security Seminar." You can imagine. I and some activist friends decide to counter their conference with our own show. SOC gives us equal access to their campus. We bring in speakers, too, and anti-war films, and workshops.

In my peasant blouse and unruly hair, twenty-one years old and earnest, far from worldly, I am interviewed by an immaculate woman in a Medford TV studio. "We have to question the assumptions behind the National Security Seminar," I tell her. "Do nuclear weapons and a huge defense budget *really* make us more secure? What would actual human security look like?"

I think I am a curiosity to her, but she is very nice, of course.

Surprisingly, our Human Security Seminar is a sort of hit. People do come, they listen, they talk, they ask questions. Even some of the military officers come.

And on the strength of this project, I'm invited to a gathering later that year at a lodge on the McKenzie River near Eugene. Leslie Gray, a philanthropist, wants to give away a big chunk of money. She's invited a bunch of community activists (I'm the youngest) to decide how to use that money to seed social change in Oregon. We decide to start a foundation: the McKenzie River Gathering Foundation. I jump on board with both feet.

I serve on the grantmaking board for several years. Because I don't have a particular axe (racial justice, nuclear power, farmworkers, peace, gay rights) to grind, like most of the other activists on the board, I become a listener, a space, a facilitator of meetings. I feel useful and deeply heartened by the nitty-gritty work of the groups we give grants to.

However, that question about the point of most leverage never lets go of me. I think a lot about Frederick Buechner's phrase—"the place where your deep gladness meets the world's deep need."

DREAMWORK AND SOCIAL CHANGE

In my forties, when I discover Jeremy Taylor, I am drawn to the way he recognizes dreamwork as a force for social change.

His first insight into how this might happen came about when he was a conscientious objector during the Vietnam War, and found himself assigned to run a group in Oakland called "Overcoming Racism" for white activists who had been asked to leave their civil rights work because of their arrogance and unconscious racism.

The group almost folded because the activists were so defensive. Finally, almost by accident, Jeremy asked them to talk about their dreams. (He and his wife Kathryn had been wrestling with sexism in their young marriage by working on their dreams.) What if he asked these people to share their "racist" dreams—of menacing groups of Black teenagers, etc.?

Thus began, as he says, an "open-ended exploration of the symbols of racial stereotypes." As they began to see that these dream images were symbolic of repressed and unacceptable parts—"dark," scary parts—of themselves, they began to take their projections back off their Black neighbors. Eventually they changed so much that they were welcomed back into the work.

In *Where People Fly and Water Runs Uphill*, Jeremy writes, "I am now completely convinced that the universal phenomenon of repression and projection is the root psychological cause of all racism. . . . Denying aspects of our own unconscious, natural human makeup makes denial of the humanity of others inevitable." After this first revelatory foray into group dreamwork, he began to offer dream groups all over the place, including psychiatric hospitals and San Quentin prison.

This story is medicine for me. I feel heartened, comforted, excited as I read it. What if dreamwork—my deep gladness—could be a way to address the world's deep need?

This kind of dreamwork could help us, I believe, to heal our relationship to the Earth. Because, of course, we do not only project our fears onto each other. We project them into the ground. We cast our distrust of the fierceness, sexuality and wildness of our emotions and bodies onto the planet itself, allowing us to treat her in brutal, exploitative ways. We have got to learn to look inward with curiosity and mercy, or we will be goners. If we owned our own mistakes, fears, and wildness we would look around us with entirely different eyes.

I HEAR A VOICE

Southern Oregon and Portland
1978
24 years old

I've left Ted and am living in Ashland. I've started dating Paul the co-counseling teacher, who lives in Eugene, a hundred miles away. My dad calls one October night and says, "Are you sure you don't want to go to college?"

He's now a professor at Lewis and Clark College in Portland and his kids can go for free.

Yes, by god, I do!

Two months later I'm enrolled, bounding through my courses like a dog rolling in the snow. Reading *The Faerie Queene* and *Middlemarch*. Taking aikido, learning to fall and extend ki. Writing poetry. I'm six years older than my classmates, which makes me six years more grateful to be in school.

At first I stay with my dad in his new wife's tidy formal house. I love having oatmeal with him at a café every morning as we commute to the college, but the wife doesn't like having me around, and after a few months I move out, to share a big old Portland house with three other young working people.

Lying one night in the bathtub of that big house, floating in warm water, I feel a false floor give way inside me. My heart opens. I suddenly feel capable of being serious about someone, instead of being that tumbleweed, that flitting butterfly.

But who? Ted? Paul? Ted still loves me, and that connection is still alive inside me somewhere too. And Paul has been so good for me, though I'm intimidated by his clarity, and I'm not the woman of his dreams, so I'd have to get over that somehow.

There's one more possibility: Ted's best friend, Sam, one of the woodworkers we lived with in the pear-orchard house in Medford. He's moved to Portland to expand his loom-building business. I'm attracted to him but it would be nuts to pursue it. First, because he's Ted's best friend. And second, because he already has a girlfriend, Jenny, in architecture school back East. I've met her and like her—she's grounded and clear-eyed.

In spite of all the counseling I've done with Paul, all those hours of tears I've shed, I'm far from rational yet. I make the crazy choice.

Sam is chubby and dark-haired, owlish. A deep-feeling intellectual, clever with his hands. Wrote his college thesis on James Joyce, always has a book in his pocket. Smokes. Wealthy, alcoholic parents. He tells me about hiding in a closet, trying to shield his younger brother while his parents raged. I'm ready to surrender to someone, and I do. Our first moment holding hands is electric, almost terrifying. I fall like a stone, into some wild tundra or savannah of my soul.

Bang! Here comes the cold. And the breathing memories reappear, more intense than they'd ever been. This is their third visit. Argenta, then Norway. And now, again, deep and sur-prising—though still subtle—quiet as alpenglow.

One afternoon in my sunny room in Portland, I lie in bed drinking in the sweetness of this amazing thing. I've called in sick from work (a teaching internship for which I get college credit) and have nothing better to do than to feel this mysteri-ous stream of whatever-it-is.

Suddenly a male voice speaks. Not familiar, but strong, with a lot of personality. I don't know "where" I hear him—in my head, or in the room. Both, maybe.

He says, "You're in the first level of deep childhood."

Okay, I think. Cool. This experience has a name—an actual name. Deep childhood.

But as the sun sets and the room darkens I start to wonder.
Who was that guy?
How did he know what was going on in my head?
What is "the first level?" Is that the strongest level, or the faintest?
And—since it has a name—it must happen to other people, right? Who?

Lying there with my cold, I am happy to know that someone

in the invisible world is keeping an eye on me. It is comforting. So odd. But wonderful.

Back to Sam. We care for each other for a few marvelous months. He keeps saying that it's over with Jenny, that they both know it, they just haven't officially called it off. But June comes and Jenny arrives from Boston. Sam's dad, a big-shot lawyer, disapproves of me (not that he's ever met me). He found Jenny a summer internship in Portland so she and Sam could be together, and Sam didn't tell her not to come.

I am rent, torn down the middle like a piece of old silk. How could he? After how utterly I fell for him, what we had together, how could he let her come? But there she is! A few blocks away, in his house, in his bed! I get pneumonia. Sick as a parrot. Coughing, broken hearted. I go home so my mother can take care of me, and take a heavy course of antibiotics. After the course of medication is done, I'm better but not well. The meds fixed something but made no dent in my actual wound.

At home again in my house, I lie like a lost sock looking out my little attic window, trying to get better.

And I have a dream.

FROG STORM — *Dream*

1977
24 years old

A man finds himself caught in a terrible thunderstorm. Frogs pop up all over the muddy road. He takes shelter in an underground cavern, where pools of black water ringed with crystalline ice glimmer in the dark. The storm rages underground as well. Cracks of thunder and lightning fill the cavern.

The next day, I find myself sitting up in bed, madly writing. The dream has prompted a story, called "A Frog-Dream." The plot is simple:

> A sick man collapses in a clearing in the forest. A woman tends him in her hut. While he is unconscious, he explores the pools in an underground cave, and realizes the pools reflect different versions of him—a slave dealer, a man wrestling a bear, and so on. One pool shows a frog, and he chooses that pool to dive into. He emerges, healed, lying in the dry streambed near the woman's hut.

The story ends with the man and woman heading upstream to find out why the streambed is dry. We don't find out what happens next; that is evidently for another story. But when I put down my pen after three days of writing, I am well. I get up, I breathe, my life-force has kicked back on. What the antibiotics could not take care of, a run of creative activity has cured. The nippy labor of feeling my way into a mythic dimension of my problem, and writing a positive ending to the story, has given me my first heady taste of the healing power of storytelling.

When Sam finally tells Jenny about us, at the end of the summer—and she flies, grieving, back to Boston—I am up in my attic room waiting for him. I have stayed helplessly faithful to the untamed spacious place I had fallen into, but we don't know how to heal what has just happened. He tells me that it had been a test; he's known me for years, including my habit of alighting and blowing away.

I don't know how to get mad at him. And I can't break up with him *now*, because I feel so guilty about Jenny and what this has cost her. I can't talk about any of it, and neither can he.

In our respective families we haven't learned to talk; haven't learned how to do anything but duck into a closet, be hammered by our feelings, come out and soldier on. Though we stay together a couple more years, we never quite find our way back to each other. The wonder of our initial months together, which produced that incredible run of deep childhood, is ground to powder under the weight of what we can't say.

THREE

What would I have said, if I could?

Hey, Sam! That was horrible for Jenny—but it was just as horrible for me. You done me wrong, there, buddy. Not admitting you were still involved with her; not telling her about me before she came; stringing us both along all summer. Sleeping with her and coming over in the evening to reassure me that you loved me!

I really loved you, obviously. I didn't give up even through all of that shit. And I still love you, I think. But I've learned something.

No, not your turn yet, I have more to say.

Part of me thinks I have to stay with you now because we've already paid such a high price. But another part knows that is a stupid reason to stay.

I learned a couple of things from this.

First, don't get involved with someone who is still in a relationship. I'm so sorry I did that. If a guy says, "It's over, we just haven't declared it," I'll back away slowly with my hands in the air. I made a big mistake there, and I feel ashamed.

Also, I'm worthy of better treatment. Not to be lied to out of cowardice. Not to be "tested" in that way.

So, in spite of how guilty I feel, and how hard I fell for you back in the winter, I think we'd better call this off. I thought I was ready for commitment, but now I suspect not. I need to be single for a couple of years. Give myself a rest, stop bouncing around, see who I am under my own skin.

You know that Frog-Dream story I wrote—which ends with the couple heading upstream to find out what's blocking the flow of that river? I don't need a man for that, I guess; I can finish that fairy tale on my own. It's a river inside me, after all.

***

Alas, the girl who could have said that is not the girl I was.

I thought I had to have a man, someone to shield me from the cold wind blowing through a father-shaped hole in my heart. I couldn't imagine breaking my pattern by staying single. That never occurred to me. The best I could imagine was to *make* myself stay with someone.

This whole nine-month adventure, from the bathtub moment in November when I felt the false floor give way to the end of August when Jenny left—through the Voice, the pneumonia, the dream and fairy tale, the anguish—was a watershed time for me. I was a sadder but wiser girl after that. I began to operate less on the fuel of fear and more on the fuel of guilt. I was yanking on those harsh reins. I did slow down, gradually, but the force behind my choosing and staying was nothing like delight or longing.

I grieve now for that young woman who just did not love herself very well.

WINDING DOWN

Portland, Oregon
1979
26 years old

My dad divorces his grumpy new wife and moves across town to live with his friend David in a tall raggedy old Victorian in Southwest Portland. A brilliant redhead, Mary, lives in a matching Victorian next door, and eventually they join up. Sam and I take my dad's place as David's roommates, and we all work on fixing up the old houses. I sheetrock and paint an upstairs bedroom and make it into a bookbinding studio. Sam, in one of his finer moments, takes a jackhammer to the driveway and makes a backyard for the two houses.

I finish college, get a credential to teach high school English, and spend a terrible few months teaching at Beaverton High School—150 kids a day and no classroom of my own, just a cart with books that I drive through the halls. I quit with relief at the end of the year. I will have to teach in a different kind of school, where I can know my students.

Sam and I are winding down. He's drinking more, flirting with the barmaid (who he later marries), and we continue to not-talk.

As luck would have it, Kim, the tall rainbow-and-shadow artist who I copied out *The Golden Key* for—my first great love—belongs to a printmaking studio across the street. I run into him often, always with a lurch in my stomach. I start to face the scalded, sealed-off part of me that still loves him. I haven't begun to heal that loss. I am riven, shaken, chilled as I realized how deep it goes, my belief that I've blown my chance at true love. I write about it in my journal. Sam reads it. *Such* a dumb idea.

I finally stop Kim one day outside his studio and tell him I have something to say.

"I still love you. I don't know how it happened, or what to do about it, but I've never stopped being in love with you."

He says, "No." He looks humbled, doubtful, surprised. "Really?"

I show him the pages in my journal. He stands on the sidewalk with the paper in his hand and stares down at me.

I can see that he believes me. He looks at me, worry and kindness in his big dark eyes. He doesn't know what to say.

HAWKEYE

She does cram a lot of life
into her life. Oh, dear.
How long will it take her
to unpack her twenties?

And what will she do about Kim?
She still can't ignite for herself
what he ignited in her.
Can we help her with that?

We are. That glimpse of storytelling as medicine
after her pneumonia crisis
came straight from us.

And now she knows about deep childhood.

Well, not much about it. She knows the name.

She knows someone is looking out for her.
I don't know. She forgets so fast.
She wonders, anyway.
It's a start.

She is hungry to learn. And she has us.
She'll find her way.

FOUR

In which I want to have children

BETWEEN LIVES

1981
28 years old

My mom moves out of her rose-ceilinged house in the city onto two hillside acres in Newberg, south of Portland. Her windows look south over a valley full of filbert orchards and sunlight. She and her sister Barb start a little restaurant in downtown Newberg called The Sage. Now, however, she's been offered a job teaching English in a refugee camp in the Philippines.

I'm twenty-eight years old and perched between lives — done with college, done with Sam, looking for a teaching job. This leaves me free to take over my mom's life while she goes to the Philippines. I move into her house and take on her role in the café. I cook whole wheat loaves every morning, chat with the regulars, count the cash at the end of the day. It smells good in there, of bran muffins and caramelized onions and coffee, and I love my cheerful Quaker aunt Barb. It's a sweet place to be.

On the romantic front, I want to get married. I'm primed to prove my commitment skills. I believe that since I've told Kim about my wound, I've healed it. I've postponed having children this long, but it's been a hunger rising in me all through my twenties.

Into this threshold moment comes a dream.

WEATHER UNDERGROUND — *Dream*

1981
28 years old

I belong to a radical political group, the Weather Underground. We are scattered all around the country, wanted by the feds. We can't communicate by any normal means, because the police will find us, so we are developing telepathy.

There is a yeasty, lucid, numinous quality to this part of the dream—a sense of developing new powers.

Then I'm in a hall with a lot of people, all going one direction. I'm going against the crowd in the other direction, struggling upstream, the only one going the other way.

WEATHER UNDERGROUND — *Reflection*

> *Because of a necessity, man acquires organs.*
> *Therefore, necessitous one, increase your need.*
> —Rumi

This dream taught me something I would not otherwise ever know. I know what it *feels like* to have a superpower. To grow a new organ, a capacity that is latent in me but not developed. It stretched me into higher, finer territory. The feeling of "leveling up" rings in my soul somewhere to this day, like the sound of a bell that never quite fades out.

This is one of the core dreams of my life. It reassures me that it is, has been, will be, *worth it*: all my confusion, moving every year, never taking the easy way. The dream lets me know—heartfully, in my chest and belly and cheeks—that something precious and magical will be born from the struggle.

HAWKEYE

Yes, honey. This is just how powers inside you are turned on.
This is a taste, a whiff.
Increase your need.

Off goes my mom to her refugee camp in Bata'an to work with boat people from Vietnam and Laos. I ride my bike to work at the café, join an Irish dance troupe, read poetry, and long for children.

My sister Barbara and her boyfriend bought (with my mother's help) a tiny white house next door to my mother, looking out over the sunny valley. In the weedy field below their house, a guy named Ben puts up a teepee. I know him, sort of; he's a friend of friends in Portland. Stocky, amiable, blond. He drives his rattly VW bug past our house every day, but it is a month before I can entice him into our house to have blueberry muffins and watch TV. We sit together on the couch and watch *To Serve Them All My Days* on PBS. It's cold in that teepee, and I'm a very good cook. He's done for.

He comes in his VW to pick me up one icy night after I've closed up the restaurant. In the dark parking lot behind the Sage he asks, "Do you want to go steady?" I laugh and say yes.

"I was reluctant to start seeing you," he admits, "because what if it didn't work out? And there you are, right next door, watching me drive past with some other girl?"

We're off and running. He is easy to connect with; reads poetry, talks about his spiritual path. He's a skilled woodworker but more or less broke all the time. With two friends, he makes fine furniture in a woodshop in Portland, but they spend as much time joking and drinking coffee as building tables. He takes his showers at a downtown gym. I pay his gym membership. He is all in for getting married and having kids.

We ask the Portland Quaker Meeting to take our marriage under their care. They meet with us to see if we are ready. No one on our clearness committee asks us about money. Would we have listened if they had? We are comfortable together. He is willing. We have an engagement party.

Meanwhile I try to start a school.

I know what a rare a gift my time in Argenta was—a lucky

two years in a school so intimate, so supportive, so practical and spiritual. I want to create a homemade school something like that for urban high schoolers in Portland. My idea is that students could live with Quaker families in the city, and we could come together in the morning, begin each day with silence, and learn from each other. Two other teachers join me in planning and sketching out details. When I talk to the Friends Meeting in Portland about it, they decline to sponsor it. It's too much for one Meeting to take care of, they tell me—it should be under the care of the Yearly Meeting, the entire body of Quakers in the Northwest. So I drive around and talk to people all over Oregon and Washington, and cheer the project on. It would be a school based on loving connection, on Quaker values of simplicity and integrity.

LIVE UP TO THE LIGHT

A young woman in the Meeting room starts to sing, her clear voice buoyed by the deep listening of 200-plus Quakers.

> *Live up to the light, the light that thou hast,*
> *And more will be granted thee;*
> *Live up to the light, and remember my child,*
> *You are never alone—no never—*
> *So live up to the light thou hast.*

Tears run hot down my cheeks. My head hurts, my heart hurts, I'm shaking with disappointment and embarrassment. I've just exposed my dream of starting a little school to the people I need help from. I'm at Yearly Meeting—the annual gathering of Quakers in the Northwest. It's a kind of week-long camp. We chat and worship and folk dance but also consider business, such as whether to sponsor a homemade high school.

The assembled gathering has said no.

For a worthy reason: we should support public schools. But in the course of the heavy-handed discussion about the merits of private versus public education, my bright-flowering twig— my open-hearted wish to give back to the world what Argenta gave to me—is clipped. It falls to the floor of the room, unseen.

At twenty-nine I don't really have the stamina to run a school, and my elders maybe sense that. I have the vision, and the humane skills to teach and administer, but not the staying power. I don't know it, though, and in the silence following the decision, I am devastated.

Then the young woman begins to sing. *"Live up to the light, the light that thou hast . . ."* She sings right to me, letting me know I am not alone. The twig has not fallen unregarded to the floor. I *have* been seen.

When we shake hands and the silence ends, friends and strangers come up and hug me, hold me, and I am comforted.

Still, the work I want most to do in the world, the gift I have to give, is roadkill. Years of imagining, months of ground-laying, of driving around to explain the project, have been washed away. When I creep into my sleeping bag in a green dome tent on the lawn outside the meeting hall that night, I am sad and raw.

And I wake in the morning laughing.

TAP DANCING MOUSE – *Dream*

1982
29 years old

A gray mouse, in full formal dress—top hat and tuxedo—
appears out of a mousehole in the wall. He starts to dance,
waving his tiny black hat and doing an old-time fancy tap dance
with his little clickity feet. He is jaunty, proud of himself, a hell
of a dancer.

TAP DANCING MOUSE — *Reflection*

> *Don't take yourself so goddamned seriously.*
> —Ben Zander

I lie in my sleeping bag smiling while green light fills the tent. When it gets too hot, I roll out onto the lawn, dress, and go to breakfast, marveling at the speed and cleverness in the creation of this dream. Someone on the dream team in my head called down to central casting for a mouse and sent him through the wall to make me laugh.

The dream isn't just the precise cure for my trouble; it shows me that I carry my own doctor inside me, my own Saint Francis who sows joy where sadness was. "A mouse is miracle enough to stagger sextillions of infidels," said Walt Whitman. He probably didn't even know they can dance.

THE TORN RING

1984

Ben and I get married in December of 1983, under the care of Multnomah Meeting. We dance to live Irish music in the meeting room after the hour-long, silence-based ceremony. I wear a wreath of roses in my hair and a silky blue dress my mother made. It's a fun, lovely party.

We come home on Christmas break to have this party—from a school in California. When my dream of starting a school fizzled, I still wanted to work in a Quaker school. So I found us jobs at John Woolman School in Grass Valley, tucked into the dry gold foothills of the Sierra Nevada. Since Argenta Friends School closed in 1980, John Woolman is the only Quaker high school west of the Mississippi. Ben and I share the job of school cook, and I teach algebra. Not that I'm good at that; but in a small school, somebody has to.

The students love us because we make fresh bread for every dinner, a round hot loaf on each table. One night in the crowded, steamy kitchen, I throw a handful of flour onto a batch of bread dough and my wedding ring catches on a screw on the giant Hobart mixer. My ring finger, and the ring, are shredded, bloody. I go to the ER and get stitched up, and eventually the ring is repaired as well. The tiny inscription on the inside of the ring—a line from William Blake, "For everything that lives is holy"—will never be quite the same.

Ben and I have stopped using birth control. I keep my knees up after sex, and feel hopeful about being pregnant any day. One rainy February night, I have a dream.

ASK FOR HORSES — *Dream*

February 21, 1984
31 years old

I'm a young woman or girl in Central Asia, sometime in the distant past, living in a dry village surrounded by mountains. I am an apprentice or adopted daughter to a powerful older woman, a witch of some kind.

A troupe of four peddlers come riding up the mountain trail, with laden donkeys. The tall man in front is intense, scary, magical. Two giant black eunuchs follow him, dressed in silver foil loincloths, with sheathed foil swords where their erect penises ought to be. At the back walks a raggedy slight person, maybe ten or twelve years old, called the bird-girl. The peddlers roll out a big carpet in the dirt square in the center of the village, and lay out semi-spiritual trade goods—charms, salves, mirrors, jewelry—on the rug. In the evening they put on a performance, swallowing swords and fire: a kind of haunting circus.

I sit on the wall of a low round fountain, watching. I feel a tap on my shoulder and a whisper in my ear:

"Don't turn around." She pauses.

"Do you think they will give you a gift?"

I know this is the bird-girl talking. She's hiding in the water behind me so the other peddlers don't see her. I find her question very hard to answer. This is the most intense moment of the dream, this consideration.

I don't know why they would give us a gift, but . . . "No" can't be the answer—otherwise why would she ask?

"Yes," I finally say.

She is relieved, and says, "Good. They will expect you to choose something from the carpet. But they have a herd of Siberian horses off on the steppe, which are in danger of inbreeding, and they will have to give them to you if you ask. They won't like it, but they'll have to do it. *Ask for horses.*"

The girl crawls back through the water, the way she came—below the fountain's rim. I see her out the corner of my eye. She does not want the men to know that she has talked to me.

My body thrills with energy at what she has just told me, so I have to walk. I walk through the streets all night, barefoot. I never ask in the dream but wake up feeling that it is not too late.

Not to play favorites, but this is the most beautiful dream I've ever had. And possibly the most important. The jeweled, painted-Persian-miniature quality of it, and the folktale drama of the story, tugged me into a long study of the Silk Road. Because of this dream, I've spent days, hours, months, years, poring over books of pictures and maps of Central Asia. Well before Kyrgyzstan and Tajikistan entered our familiar lexicon, I was wandering in my mind along those harsh, dry mountainsides in the company of sheep, watching furious games of Buz-kashi from the sidelines, swallowing dust as the horses pounded past, or feeling the air freeze in my nostrils as I check for rubies in a glacial stream running down from some impossible pass.

I know the dream wants to be a book, with a series of bright, shadowed paintings and the punch of an old Sufi tale, but so far no. It's become an essay or two, and a long, failed novel, but not the hand-sized leather-bound volume that I imagine.

This dream comes one February night during a California rainstorm, two months after my wedding to Ben. Something is wrong with this marriage, as the torn ring might be trying to tell me, and the dream too. I've taken what is laid out on the carpet: the guy camped next door in a teepee, the ready solution to my minimized desire. I'm not asking for much—no great love, no partner with his own career, not even financial stability. A nice guy who also wants children and is willing to commit to me.

Or so I think! Our friends pool their money and give us a nice stereo as a wedding present, and as we unwrap it, Ben asks, "When we break up, who will get the stereo?"

I should have taken him by the shoulders, looked him in the eye, and asked, "What do you mean?" Not harshly, but willing to know the truth. Instead I pretend he is kidding. Ha ha.

This bothers something deep inside me, as it turns out. My soul is not interested in a shrink-to-fit life, a take-what's-laid-out-on-the-carpet life. Sure, for a decade or two I can choose that, and I do. But right at the beginning of that twenty-year descent, a seed cracks open in my heart that will keep trying to grow me up and out of myself, toward the big world and the great adventure. This dream is that seed.

The key to keeping the seed alive is how my body feels just before I say "Yes" to the bird-girl's question. Risky, open. That is the moment of truth, of suspension, when the story can go either way. I crave moments of strange difficulty like that, moments when something amazing is being offered that I can accept or refuse. I'm not naturally good at noticing this: terrible, in fact, which is why the dream comes to help me. I also begin to look around for horses, to wonder where or what they are, those sturdy, rough-haired beings who need me as much as I need them.

DREAMWORK: WHAT WE DO NOT KNOW

Dreams never come to tell us what we already know. This was one of Jeremy Taylor's maxims. Case in point: I was wildly unaware, at this point in my life, of my tendency to ask for less than I wanted, and in fact not to have any idea what I wanted. Because this problem went so deep, and was so invisible to me, it took a BIG dream to counteract it. *Ask for Horses* shone a powerful light on my failing. I'm a little surprised it wasn't a nightmare. Dreams often come as nightmares if we chronically refuse to know something, which was me all over. But this was the opposite of a nightmare.

The thing is, I was actively sharing dreams that winter, with a group of students and other teachers at John Woolman. The dream-makers didn't need to use a nightmare, because I was listening. And they had something that would reach me better: a fairy tale. Mythical characters, richly drawn paintings, and an ending full of thrilling possibility. They knew I would hold onto a story like that, lean into it, try to listen up and feel my way forward.

ALL OVER THE MAP

1984–1988
31–35 years old

Ben and I carom around the continent, moving every year. We tootle from John Woolman to a magical homemade school on the Oregon coast called Fire Mountain School. There I teach eight kids, second through sixth graders, while he works part-time in the grocery store. At the end of that fun but exhausting year I tell Ben it's his turn to get a real job. So he says, "Okay, we'll go to Alaska. I can work with my friend Matt building log houses."

We drive his VW bug, with my sister Barbara and her bull-dog, my white deaf cat Snow, and a few suitcases, up the Al-Can Highway, through the Yukon and endless miles of scrub-by spruce trees, to Fairbanks. Once we're settled, Ben peels logs with his buddies and I cook at a downtown restaurant, A Moveable Feast. It's the most civilized place in this hard-scrabble outpost. I love my job, with the smell of croissants and roasting chicken, but I feel like an alien in the frozen-earth, scraggle-tree, take-your-showers-at-the-laundromat frontier town.

There are glorious moments—dogsledding, silent and speedy through the dark forest; skiing right out the back door of our cabin; canoeing all night under the gold and pink clouds of the never-gets-dark Fairbanks summer—but one nine-month winter is more than enough.

I apply for us to work at Pendle Hill, a Quaker study center near Philadelphia. We are hired, sight unseen, and move again, another few thousand miles, with what we can fit on the plane to Pennsylvania. My dear white deaf cat Snow, who has moved with me many times, has had enough. He dies the day before we are to fly out.

When we drive our rental car up the driveway into Pendle Hill, Gwen and Elizabeth—the other cooks—run out waving brooms and rolling pins. I laugh and jump out of the car, loving them and this place right away. It is Argenta in civilized clothing. Fieldstone barns instead of rickety wooden shacks, giant beech trees instead of fir forest, bright-eyed adults instead of long-haired teenagers. But the same Quaker calmness is in the woodwork. We sit together in silence every morning, students and staff, just as we used to in the log Meetinghouse looking out at Kootenay Lake. I love this.

And, as in Argenta, we don't need a car. We cook and eat and go to movies with the same people that we sit in silence with every morning. Once again my life feels undivided. Deep childhood picks right up on my happiness and is nourished by the daily silence. I get the cold almost as soon as we arrive, and the quiet, wind-from-elsewhere memories go on for almost six months, the longest ever.

Ben and I are content in our little apartment over the library. We are both working, so I'm not worried about money. We even sign on to stay for a second year! It is such a relief not to move.

With lots of spare time, I play. I sew up all the fabric I own. Discover the power of silent retreats. Do a rare-book search (pre-internet!) for the favorite books of my childhood—oversized English books from the 1940s about Orlando the Marmalade Cat. I manage to unearth a few tattered copies. Play Scrabble with the elderly librarian, do some life modeling for the art college next door.

But I'm not the slightest bit pregnant, after four years of trying. I have a bunch of tests which reveal how scarred my insides are; then surgery which leaves me with only one not-very-good fallopian tube. And a knot of grief in my gut. Our best friends Janet and Gabriel, who are also on staff and live across the hall, have a baby while we're there. They are generous in letting me hold the baby. Janet is joyful at being a mother, and I am sad.

Gabriel is one of the few people I've ever met with the same sense of play as me. He takes me tree climbing, up to the tip of a very tall fir tree, where I perch as if at the top of a mast, swaying in the living wind. Together we put on a parade, with all the students and staff, just for fun. We dress up, make flags and music, and march around the buildings singing. Gabriel is, like me, a lifelong Quaker. His parents work at the same Friends boarding school in Barnesville, Ohio, that my mother went to. It was a joyful home for her, exactly as Argenta was for me. These Quaker harmonies make a friendly, easy resonance between us.

Meanwhile, back in Oregon a couple of surprising things happen.

First, a winter conversation.

We go home to see our families in Portland for a couple of weeks at Christmas. While we're there, my old love Kim, the rainbow-and-shadow artist whose absence still haunts me—calls up out of the blue and invites Ben and me to come for tea. We walk over on a wet, dark afternoon, the street smelling of rain and fir trees. I wonder what's up. I've never been to Kim's house, nor met his wife Mary.

We hang up our coats and Mary brings tea.

Kim, lean, tall, bright-eyed, sits across the table. He holds up a book called *We* by Robert Johnson.

"Have you read this?"

"No." We shake our heads.

"It's the story of Tristan and Iseult. Do you know the story?" I nod; Ben says no. Kim recounts the tragic love affair, and then holds the book up again.

"Robert Johnson is a Jungian, and he's using this myth to look at the archetype of romantic love. And when I read it I realized something."

He looks at me across the table. "When you and I were together, it was not a regular kind of relationship. Not the kind where you could make a daily life together. It was an archetypal thing. You helped me to connect with my *anima*—my feminine soul—and I did something like that for you, with your *animus*, the male aspect of you. That's what we were for each other."

He shows us around their house: his etchings, Mary's mother's quilts, and we hug goodbye.

We walk the few blocks back to my dad's house in darkness, the mist fluffing my hair. I am reeling with astonishment.

How did he know I needed that? How desperately I needed to hear that I mattered to him, down in the legendary territory where he mattered to me? That I had not made it up, that I was not deluded, that we had in truth been wine and firelight for each other?

An old hard place in my breastbone melts. With one generous, intuitive conversation, Kim has given me back the sacred quality of our connection, to replace the confusion and shame I've carried for fifteen years.

The other thing happening in Oregon is a house. Ben and I, while we career from California to Alaska to Pennsylvania, have picked up the payments on the little white house next to my mother, the very land where Ben had pitched his teepee when I was wooing him with muffins. My sister Barbara and her boyfriend abandoned it, and my mom asked if we wanted to buy it. It has walls like cardboard, but the view is fantastic. While we move around, we rent it to my other sister, Kathryn, and her husband, Tim, while she finishes college.

But Kathryn has graduated, and they're moving to Vermont.

The wanderer in me raises her tired head: *A home?* I'm thirty-five years old and have moved at least thirty-five times, as the *Moon Man* dream seemed to know I would. The prospect of living in my own house is a pull strong enough to override everything, even my Pendle Hill happiness. So Ben and I don't sign contracts for a third year. We pack our suitcases, buy plane tickets for Portland.

Three days before our flight I take Gabriel out for tea, in a café near Pendle Hill. He is my dear friend. I've been dreaming about him for months but have tried to ignore the dreams. Now it seems like it might be safe to say something, since we're about to go. I lean over the teacups, across the glass table.

"I just wanted to tell you, before I go, that I've been

dreaming about you for months. But it didn't seem right to say it. I waited until just before we left so there wouldn't be time for things to get weird."

I feel like I'm handing him something tender, a small gift. I'm not asking for anything. Just think somehow that he should know.

He looks at me, looks at his tea, looks up again. "I told Janet a few days ago that I thought I was in love with you."

Oh, no no no. No no. The possibility that he loves me, too, has—no kidding—not occurred to me. He reaches over and takes my hand.

Three days, it turns out, is plenty of time for things to get weird. We kiss under the giant beech tree. I feel a slow sense of explosion, erupting in shaking sobs. I'm being stirred with a bloody spoon. We are both married, I'm leaving, it is beyond hopeless, and yet some great aliveness, an uplifting stream of desire and assent, is pouring through me.

I somehow get on the plane. As we sit in our seats waiting for takeoff, I tell Ben: "If I still feel like this in six months, I'm coming back."

But I don't, of course. Instead, I get a scorching letter from Janet, who found out about it after we left. Her sense of betrayal, added to my shaking heart, makes the whole thing hot and horrible. That surge of joy cost way too much.

I push the whole thing behind me. Get a job as a cook in Portland. Make curtains. Unpack books. Look out over the valley of filbert trees. And I have a dream.

GOD AS A COW – *Dream*

October 1988
35 years old

God is a cow. She "dries up" and is in pain if I don't come faithfully to milk her. She tosses me on her long horns; she is angry because I am so irresponsible and come only when I feel like it.

A great hand, like an angel's hand, reaches out and catches me as I am tossed away.

Back on the farm in southern Oregon, when I was milking the Jersey cow, I would never have dreamed of sleeping through a milking. I knew it would be terrible for her if I didn't come to relieve her of her sixteen pounds of milk each morning. I showed up, at dawn, every day. She was a warm, living creature who counted on me.

It never occurred to me that God is like that.

I didn't much try to picture God, but if I did, I guess I imagined something like a river. A source of nourishment that is always there. I could go down to the bank — or not — and dip in my tin cup. If I didn't go, it didn't bother the river. It was my loss only.

But I see it all differently after this dream.

It is *never* "just for myself." It's *always* a relationship: God *is* the relationship, the sacred showing-up: a Being or a space that is both inside and outside me, whose emergence is mysteriously dependent on me. I can't just come and go as I please, and expect to be nourished by the sacred. It doesn't work that way.

In the morning after this dream, I sit with my tea, thinking about it. I wonder if I can change. Here in my little white thin-walled house, I recall how much I love sitting in silence every morning, how precious those daily meetings at Pendle Hill and Argenta were to me. But can I do this just for me? Sit in silence every morning?

This dream says it matters. Show up.

It makes instant sense to me.

But I can't seem to do it. For years, I hold this dream over myself and try to start a daily meditation practice. It doesn't work. It's not until ten years later, when I start to write a poem every morning, that I finally feel in my body the beautiful absorption of milking that cow.

At some point I see another, sharper message in the dream, related to the affair I didn't quite have with Gabriel. The long horns hint at an unfaithful wife: shades of Shakespeare. I was not showing up for Ben (who, long before that evening in the café with Gabriel, had told me he was in love with someone else, urg).

I didn't really show up for Gabriel, either. I was clueless enough not to realize I was in love with him. It was ridiculous to think I could tell him about my dreams three days before we left without making a big mess. And not to guess that he might love me, too! It all shows how poorly I was listening. Being tossed on God's horns was a nice crackle of cosmic punishment for not paying attention.

As I recalled this dream over the years, I only remembered the cow and her horns. I internalized a fierce, clear, rather scary message: what I do, *or fail to do*, matters—whether I know it or not—so shape up!

But while writing this book I go back and reread the original record of the dream. Hmm.

An angel catches me. I am saved, salvaged, held.

The story ends with kindness.

But I forget that part of the dream for so long.

Why?

Because I felt guilty. My emotional grooves ran toward wincing and cringing at the memory of mistakes. I didn't have much practice in forgiving myself, or even seeing that that might be a good idea.

A SAD THING

1989–1990

One morning, about a year after we return from Pendle Hill, Ben and I are having toast and scrambled eggs before we leave for work. He leans back with his coffee and says, "I'm moving into Portland. You can come if you want to."

My heart sinks. "What about living in our own house? That's why we moved home!"

"I know, but I can't stand the commute. The twenty stoplights in Tigard. I'm done with it. We're both working in Portland. Our friends all live there. It doesn't make sense."

My chest caves in, my shoulders curl and tighten. This feeling is lonely, heavy, and familiar—the next wave of a slow-motion body slam. Of course, he is going to move whether I do or not. And of course I'll move into town with him. I'm not going to let go that easily. Our friends do live there, especially Peg and Fred, who we have become very close to in this last year, since their ten-month-old daughter, Annalee, died. It would be good to be near them. But I don't want to move again, I really don't.

A few months later Ben sits me down on the orange couch in our rented house in the city and says, "I know our marriage is over, but I'm not going to leave; I'm going to stick around until you know it, too."

"No, it isn't!" I say. "We can make this work."

I push my hurt down into my gut, feeling that slow-motion punch again. I look at his kind, square face and think, *It can't be over. Didn't we get **married**?*

We shuffle along more or less as before. He flirts with the barmaid Dory and keeps talking about her. I ride my bike back and forth to work at Portland State, join a writing group, and try not to think about what Ben said.

But a month or so later we are at the beach with Peg and Fred. Sitting on the toilet, I double over with knife-blade abdominal pain. I go to the doctor in Portland, who does an ultrasound. Oh god! I am pregnant! But her face is thin with worry.

"Don't go home," she says. "Go straight to the hospital. Have someone bring your clothes."

When the surgeon cuts out the cluster of bloody cells that is never going to be a baby, he also removes the fallopian tube it was stuck in. After my infertility surgery in Pennsylvania, that is the only tube I have.

That's it. No baby, ever.

I have six weeks off from work to recover. I need it—and more.

I am stunned. We don't have the money to adopt, and there is that business of Ben telling me our marriage is over. Peg, who we comforted after the death of her baby, tries to comfort me, but I feel lost.

I spend my days sitting up in bed in the pale winter sunlight, depressed and typing.

ORANGE TREE – *Dream*

Fall 1989
36 years old

A fairy-tale garden with a high wall around it contains a magic orange tree. A thief comes to steal the fruit, and a guard is set to catch the thief.

For months I've been working on a fantasy novel called *Orange Tree* based on this scrap of a dream. I write the story to find out what happens. Who stole the oranges, and why? I love finding out, watching the adventure unfold as I write.

My time off after the ectopic pregnancy gives me time to finish it. On a chilly day in March the hero, Shag, steps out of his home world into the world of the Presences, the mysterious beings who planted the original healing orange tree. His astonished appearance in this bigger world gives me the shivers.

I type the last sentence, close the laptop, and float around the house in a field of delight.

The creative pilgrimage of writing the novel has been true medicine. My delight is real enough. But I mistake that delight for evidence that I am okay. I push the override button and shove the mess down one more time.

Mother's Day comes. I lie on my back in bed, a slab of grief, staring at the high ceiling. Ben is nowhere to be seen.

When he comes home he says, "I bought a car!" He is jubilant. "I realized I didn't have to consult you."

I let it sink in over the next day, like gravel in my blood. Fuck. It really *is* over. In every way that counts, he's gone.

I move out to a friend's house. I take my clothes, leave him the furniture —including the wedding-present stereo. We hug goodbye, amicable as ever.

But somewhere in the move I lose my ring of spare keys.

Two weeks later I go into a small auto shop to get a new key made. Jack, the tall blue-eyed young man who owns the shop, builds me a key. I watch as he teases his employees, all older than him. He is relaxed and—here's the thing—he loves what he is doing. He moves through his work like an otter flowing down a riverbank. After Ben, who easily got tired of working, Jack's ease draws me like a flame. I go back to his shop a week or so later, trying to catch him when his employees aren't around. Leaning against a counter, I ask if he'd like to go out for coffee sometime.

He looks startled, then amused.

"I don't drink coffee," he says. "But maybe you'd like to come down and watch the Rose Festival Parade next weekend? It goes right past the shop."

"Sure!"

This lanky mechanic, who has moved only once in his life, feels like a harbor. We go for walks, dance in the kitchen, start sleeping together. For the first time in my life I stop chewing my fingernails.

I've been seeing Jack for about two months. One night, I have dinner with Peg and Fred and come over to his place afterwards.

"We made margaritas," I mention as I get undressed.

"You did what?" His face suddenly has a clamped, frozen look. I put my shirt back on.

"We had enchiladas, and margaritas."

"I thought you didn't drink."

"I hardly ever do. Like I told you, I've never been drunk in my life."

"You have to promise me that you will never drink alcohol again." He glares.

"What? Why?"

I'm so confused. I had a nice time with my friends. I probably drank half a margarita. I can't find the problem. What is he so upset about?

"If you want to be with me, I need to be sure that you will never drink alcohol."

This is not the playful, cheerful man I've been kissing. His sharp, rigid voice, and the fear—or is it fury?—of his demand puzzle and shock me. Not only does it seem unlike him, it's unlike anyone I know. My friends, my family, would never act like this. We have always let each other run free, make our own mistakes.

"What *are* you talking about? Alcohol is not an issue for me. Among my friends, I drink the least of anyone. And it's my decision—it's not up to *you* to tell me whether I'm going to have a glass of wine."

"You have to promise."

He won't let go. He clamps his jaw in sullen insistence, sure that he is in the right; I walk around the room shaking, rattled. *What is really going on here?*

He's told me that his mother drinks, and his father, who is dead, drank hard until he stopped cold turkey when Jack was four. What happened to that little boy that left him so scared,

I wonder?

I walk around pulling at my hair. *Whatever happened, he has no right to . . . Something is very wrong . . . What is really going on here?*

But I have already decided that he is a harbor.

So I tell myself: *Well, I hardly drink anyway. I don't really care about that—and he cares so much. I can be the bigger person and give him what he obviously wants so badly.*

"Okay, I promise."

Of course, what I am giving up is not alcohol at all.

WHAT??

Taking up with Jack was probably the nuttiest move I ever made. We were violently mismatched—though I didn't slow down long enough to find that out.

I'd been separated from Ben for less than a month. What was I thinking?

Well, I wasn't thinking.

My body was full of the smoke of the collapse of my marriage, and the painful ectopic end to my dream of getting pregnant—but I couldn't breathe that smoke or walk into the fire of grief behind it. It was too much, too sad. I kept running my old program: Push the override button. Play through the pain.

I still longed to be a mother. The ache for children that had driven me to marry Ben eight years earlier still drove me, somewhere below sound, and that longing refused to go away, even though I was officially infertile now. I was a fish that had been yanked out of the lake, and was gasping to be put back into water, some water, any water, no matter how clear or muddy.

Being with Jack was a relief. He was a counterweight to Ben—he loved his work, he didn't move around, he wasn't in debt. There was a solidity to him that I needed. And a physical joy and buoyancy that was very attractive. I had no idea I was desperate; I thought I was sane, capable, tracking. I was taking action on my own behalf—going back to his shop to ask him out! Good for me!

I'd moved too many times, been running too long. I was far more sad than I knew.

HAWKEYE

Oh dear. Here we go.

Honey, we get it.
You're exhausted from moving.
You want children with every bone
in your body.
So you jump from the frying pan
into the volcano.

At least you can still jump! You can still
throw yourself in.
You can increase your need and, boy, you do.

Speaking of which,
when you sent out your need
to Kim, he heard it.
He came through for you to heal that wound.
How did he know it still needed healing?
You told him in the invisible world.
He responded
and that is Magic of the Heart.

We'd like to warn you about Jack
but there are blessings you cannot imagine
embedded in that catastrophe.

We've got you. We love you. Hold on.

FIVE
In which I find children

STARS AND DROP OF WATER – *Dream*

May 3, 1994
40 years old

There is a woman, a mathematician. She is working with frac-
tals—elaborate beautiful designs. She has an enemy, but as time
goes on she realizes that his purpose in her life is to get her to
rally her forces, to grow stronger.

Then I am her, or she is me, and we start to expand out into
space. I leave the surface of the Earth and go out deep into the
stars, farther and farther, until I am either very vast or very far
away or both. I feel the enormity and blue darkness of space:
a powerful, endless feeling, a great encompassing, a great size.
I am among stars, and maybe I am a star. At the same time I
feel a deep tenderness for the Earth. Then I begin to shrink, to
go back to Earth. There is a rush of return. At the surface of
the planet I feel a gulp, a slight gathering of energy. Then I am
inside the Earth, going down, down, smaller and smaller, until
I am a drop of water. I stop. The drop is somewhere—on a
rock inside the Earth—and that is as far as I need to go.

I wake from this dream in front of a wooden bookcase, in a condominium in Chicago. I've been living with Jack for a couple of years, and we are driving across the country to visit my aunts and uncles in New Hampshire. We've stopped in Chicago to collect his friend George. George's parents recently died and he wants to come along on our adventure.

I see the bookcase as soon as we walk in the door, and it draws me like a magnet. George's dad had collected books — and dear god! What books! I pull a couple out and touch the endpapers, the gilding, the warm soft paper, the fine tooling of the spines. There are about forty volumes in the case: eighteenth- and nineteenth-century copies of Dickens and Milton and Pepys, bound by craftsmen at the top of their game — a game far beyond anything I ever learned.

My heart is in my mouth as I offer to buy ten of them for $400. It's all I have in the bank.

"Sure," George says. He's sold most of his parents' furniture and is happy to skip the hassle of finding a book dealer. "Just don't tell me how much you sell them for."

"I'm not going to sell them. I'm going to own them."

I'm not much for ownership of things generally, and since I move so often I don't tend to gather worldly goods, so this is a new feeling . . . as if I'll be a better person, more of a real person, if I own these glorious books. Amazed at my luck, I roll out my sleeping bag in front of the bookcase.

That rush of joy follows me into sleep and kindles this astronomical dream. As in that Danish observatory years before, my love of stars and books collides and swings my soul out into space.

Going out *so far* and returning to go inside the Earth — changing scale in that way, from human to star to water drop — is an indescribable experience of expansion, belonging, wonder, strangeness.

The dream also reminds me that an enemy can serve an

important purpose: to make me step up, rally my forces, get stronger. This echoes the *Weather Underground* message about increasing my need. I don't know why the dream is telling me this right now, but I'm willing to bank that information.

In time this dream becomes a poem. My manifesto, you could say.

I THANK THE EARTH FOR THINKING ME UP

What about that dream
of being something like a star,
a fiery being, out among
shining giants, in fields of light?
Or that night I turned into
a fir tree, drinking
what I needed from sky
and ground?

Those ventures
into other worlds
crave to be forged into offerings.
Our daily language longs
to be burned
until poems gleam like coins
in the warm ash.

Earth labored
a long long time
to bring into being
the zebra,
the night-blooming cereus,
and also us: our nimble hands and fluid film of words.
We don't take this seriously enough.

Let me live as if it were my work
to thank the Earth

for calling me forth. Didn't
she dream of being known
through these halting poems?
Didn't she fashion me
of leaves and mud so I could
stand on the grass and see?

Let me live in a rage of gratitude,
a sheet of vision
that falls over and over into cedar tree and star.
Let me tear myself
into rags of praise.

Back home in Portland, the old books take their place in
the glass-front bookcase that Jack and I bring back from my
grandparents' house in New Hampshire on our road trip.
When George visits us later that summer he brings me the rest
of his dad's collection, for another $400.

They glow behind the glass, giving off that heart-stopping
old-leather library smell whenever I crack open the bookcase
door. Buried treasure.

SMALL WILD BOOK – *Dream*

August 1994
40 years old

I'm teaching a bookbinding class. It is Friday. I've been teaching all week and have another class to teach today. But I need to do some prep. The students are arriving. I need to keep them busy for a few minutes while I go cut up some paper, so I create a quick assignment.

"Write a forty-five-word story with a horse in it. We'll make them into twelve-page books, with four words to a page and one word on the last page."

I give them thirty minutes to write their stories.

In 1845 Elias Howe was trying to invent a mechanical sewing machine, plugging away at the problem, getting poorer by the day. Then he had a nightmare in which he was captured by cannibals who were dancing around him with spears—and the spears had holes in the tips. He woke up sweating, and as he pictured the dream he saw the solution to his problem: make a hole in the *point* of the needle! Not the top end, where handsewing needles have it. His invention, which he patented in 1846, made him a rich man.

I'm no inventor, but at the moment of this dream I've also been immersed in a creative stream. I've been teaching bookbinding to teachers for three weeks straight. The fun of carving linoleum blocks and dropping colored inks into trays of carrageenan, of showing my students how to sew signatures and skive leather has tilled my maker's mind. When the class ends, my mind and body are still warm with artistic momentum. The flywheel is turning. Thus this dream.

I know the assignment is for me, and I do it. Here's my forty-five-word story.

SLICING THE SILENCE

Storm-dark clouds race
from the horizon, long
shadows building fast,
and out of them, gold
with black feet and
mane, a horse pours
toward us, riderless, no
sound until he is
upon us, hooves pummeling
dust and seeds, grass
blown back, and suddenly
thunder.

I bind this story into a small twelve-page book in soft brown and blue sheepskin and make a belt for it that closes with an Afghani tribal buckle, a wee silver sword. It's one of the loveliest books I've ever made. I marvel at the assignment as I work. So clear and clever—especially the way it makes the poem hammer down on the last word. The whole thing can be printed on two sheets of paper. It's more elegant than any assignment I ever came up with on my own.

It's another instance, like *Tap Dancing Mouse*, of the range of help that dreams offer. A laugh is needed? Okay. Bookbinding assignment? Here you go. Cure for lifelong habit of asking too small? On it.

P. S. The series of bookbinding classes that give birth to this dream give birth to something else.

My students are elementary school teachers, mostly women. We become friends across the table as we stitch and stamp and fold paper. I hear about their marriages and kids; they learn about my eleven-year sorrow at not being a mother.

One of these teachers has adopted children through Holt International, an agency in Eugene, and she receives adoption newsletters from them. One afternoon she turns to me and says, "You know, there are thousands of baby girls in orphanages in China. And you have to be over thirty-five and childless to adopt."

Something happens in my belly, below sound but reverberant, a temple gong from far over the ocean.

CAT-BABY — *Dream*

September 27, 1994
41 years old

Someone has a baby but doesn't intend to keep it. It's going to be raised by my Aunt Mary. When it is first brought home, it is so beautiful, small, vulnerable, pink, enchanting. It is kept for a while in a little box, inside a tiny pink plastic doll, the size of a fingernail or so. I worry about this. It would be easy to crush or lose the box.

I say, "I've heard it's good for children to be carried next to your body all the time."

Mary says, "Yes, I was raised that way."

I say, "That's why you're such a nice person, so peaceful."

She smiles but doesn't disagree.

I decide to take on this baby, keeping it next to my skin. I wish that they would give me the child to raise, for my own. I talk briefly to the mother, a golden-haired girl who does not seem too interested in it.

Some of the time the child is a young cat, with huge ears like sails. It seems feistier than a regular cat, and bigger. I carry it around and love it.

At the time of the dream Jack and I have zero plans to adopt. We are not married; we are not even talking about children. Though the gong in my belly rang when I heard the words "baby girls in China," I have not been able to talk to Jack about that in any way that he can hear.

The logjam breaks two months after the dream. Jack and I have been attending an infertility support group called Resolve, and one night in the meeting I break down sobbing. In the circle of a dozen people on folding chairs, I finally let on—to myself and to Jack—how desperate I am.

"We've been together three years, and he still doesn't get it, how bad I want this. Nothing has happened." In the circle of witnesses I finally feel safe enough to cry my truth. And the same witnesses help Jack hear it. I watch him turn on. A light kindles in his face, he puts on his hero hat and says, there and then, "We can do something about this."

It is like scrambling onto shore after almost drowning. Later I recognize this as the moment when I finally, for the first time, ask for horses.

Everything moves. A few months later, in early March, we sit in a restaurant booth with a couple who have just started an adoption agency. They work only with China. The wife is Chinese, and was herself an abandoned child during the Cultural Revolution. They have a certain zeal about getting abandoned girls out of orphanages and are eager to help us.

In April Jack and I get married in the Astoria courthouse, with random clerks for witnesses. I make a zillion trips to the small house where the adoption agency resides. We fill out forms and write a letter to the Chinese government telling them what fine parents we will be, and that we will not treat our child as a servant. By August we have a tiny photo of our skinny big-eyed daughter, and by October, less than a year after the Resolve meeting, we stand in the Seattle airport, hugging and greeting the five couples who will travel with us to China.

A few days later, we all wait, hearts in our mouths, in a room with giant purple velvet chairs in the Hangzhou Overseas Chinese Hotel. The door opens and shy teenage nannies carry in six babies. Here she is—May! A tiny girl, stick-thin and sweaty, dressed in layers of worn padded clothing and sweaters. She is six months old and weighs eleven pounds. An hour later in a noisy restaurant, she first accepts a bottle from me, sitting in my lap. This little black-haired being with searching eyes has turned me into a mother. I sit in the restaurant and cry.

The *Cat-Baby* dream came to me eight and a half months before she was born. I was clued in to the moment when her life began, thousands of miles away. When I offer, in my dream, to carry the tiny baby next to my skin, it is the beginning of my own mysterious, paperwork pregnancy.

AMAZED

1988

A sunny winter afternoon. I'm zooming up a freeway ramp in Southeast Portland, in the glow of a radiant unfamiliar happiness. I've just watched the film *Persuasion* by myself at home, and my relief when Anne and Captain Wentworth come together at the end is so intense that I feel like I've been pardoned from a crime.

As I notice this stream of joy, I get a wild glimpse of all that is going on in me. I'm driving—that complicated brightness of steering, shifting, watching. I'm planning what to do when I get to the bank. My body is breathing, making hair, pumping blood and the zillion other things that it does without my help. I'm feeling this unfamiliar joy—and I'm using some level of my mind to be aware of it all. The whole thing is a buzz of awareness so strong that it sears through me like a comet, leaving behind a glow of awe: "Isn't the mind amazing?"

ISN'T THE MIND AMAZING? — *Dream*

May 14, 1998
44 years old

I'm staying briefly at a house with a not-entirely-friendly family.

I leave to catch a train but don't know where the station is. I'm worried because I don't have my tickets. I'm going a long way.

I fly over the land, looking for the station. The countryside is beautiful, pastoral, and abstract—as if the little houses, trails, roads, trees have been changed into blocks of color. I stop on a hilltop where I find a strange machine like a video game. It's called Uncle So-and-So's Algebra Machine.

I realize I'm late for the train and say, "I'm in deep dark shit."

I start to run down a series of stairs inside the hill. I run down many flights, past rooms, doorways, pictures.

Part way down I realize I'm dreaming!

I think: "This is a dream, but it sure feels real."

I tap on the sheetrock wall of the stairwell to test it, and it is as solid as any wall in waking life.

"Wow," I say. "Isn't the mind amazing? It created this. There is no difference between this wall and a wall in my house."

I get to the bottom and find my mail. There's a package from the unfriendly family—something I left behind at their house. I open it and find a huge pink diamond. Maybe two inches long. It's a beautiful, rough pink stone, suspended in front of a plate of pearly rounded gems. It is meant for an earring, but the mount is too big—five or six inches across—and there's only one, so I decide to wear it as a pin.

Strong emotions are the ocean on which dream-ships float, or the timber from which dream-ships are built. The joy I felt sleeping in George's house in the presence of the antique books buoyed me into the wild planetary dream, into becoming both star and water drop. In the same vein, my rush of freeway amazement fuels this dream of high awareness and the pink diamond. And the root of that amazement was an intense feeling of *reprieve*.

Something to know about me: I physically participate in movies, to a surprising degree. I have been known to yell at the screen in a crowded movie theater, when a character does something I can't stand. So, that afternoon as I watch *Persuasion*, I *am* Anne, suffering her hopelessness, believing her chance at happiness has passed. And I myself am pardoned when she and Captain Wentworth realize their window to each other is still open. A whole ragged edge of my own heart is healed. A secret despair, resignation, acceptance of my fate—a sadness I wasn't even aware of—is lifted. Momentarily, but memorably.

When it lifts, I become—in the words of the dream—aware of a buried hopelessness, of being in deep shit.

Occasionally in waking life I glimpse this thread of hopelessness, but mostly it seems to run on its own code, well under conscious awareness. I'm easily manipulated by a weird, uncomfortable pressure not to make a mistake. Some part of me cringes, cowers, regrets. Taking another cue from the imagery of the dream, I often suspect that I've lost my ticket to the train, the long-distance purpose of my life.

This dream is like a zoom lens. It starts with a wide, high view, and goes down and in and down:

That it starts with flying is a wonderful omen. It's such visceral joy. I'm looking differently at my life—not at details, but at patterns.

When I land on the hillside I get a chance to begin doing inner work, symbolized by "Uncle So-and-So's Algebra

Machine"—a game like Whack-a-Mole where energy pushed down in one place appears in another, like repressed emotions. Playing this game somehow clues me in to the fact that I am in trouble. That insight sends me down, inside myself. And as I do this work, I discover that I'm dreaming. I'm creating it all. I've managed to create a solid sheetrock wall, the whole construct of my life. When I knock on it to check, I am thrilled: my mind is way more powerful than I have given it credit for.

Therein lies great hope. I am the agent here. Anything is possible.

The reward for this work, when I get all the way to the bottom of my trouble, is an astonishing jewel—which, it turns out, was mine all along.

This dream tells me, "You haven't lost anything. Not your joy, nor your long-distance purpose. The jewel of your soul is alive, waiting for you, incredibly large and beautiful. To find it you will have to first admit you are in trouble, then recognize how utterly you create the world you live in. At the bottom of that journey you will be reconnected with your diamond soul."

Possibly the diamond alleviates the need for a ticket, or even a train. I don't know. But a profound lucidity and clarity—a diamond heart—glows somewhere in the shit of my story, that I know.

It is a good thing, too. At this point in my journey I haven't admitted how oppressive my marriage to Jack is. I haven't started to run down inside the hill of my distress. I have no idea how much grief I am in for. But I thrust this dream into my pocket with the other golden dream-keys—*Weather Underground, Ask for Horses, God as a Cow*—and it encourages me. At no time in the dream do things seem dire. That sheetrock moment of awakening is a rush of wonder. And there at the base of the stairs is the great diamond, with jewels all around.

The juice of strong emotion runs both ways, into dreamland and back out again. A moment of waking lucidity can ignite a dream like this one; likewise, a powerful dream can bust open everyday reality. Ever since this dream, I look wryly at sheetrock walls. Now and again I tap on one, just to remind myself that I am capable of making it all up, and living inside my creation as if it were real. It often makes me grin.

Along these lines—sometimes nowadays I pretend to be Harold, from the children's book *Harold and the Purple Crayon*. He's a boy who draws the world with his purple crayon as he moves through it. He gets into a boat he's just drawn and sails off in it, for example. As I walk along, I hold out my hand with an imaginary purple crayon in it, and pretend to draw the sidewalk before I step on it. It's many years after the dream, but the dream has inspired me to goof around in this way. I like to remind myself that it's just possible I'm making up the world as I go along.

LYING TO THE CHINESE GOVERNMENT

1997
43 years old

Jack is after me to go back to China and adopt a sister for May.

China had been his first trip overseas, and he was like a kid in a toyshop, prowling night markets for bargains, eating tongue-burning potatoes in outdoor cafés, showing off May. A tall blue-eyed American with a Chinese baby was a crowd-attractor. He wants to go back and continue the adventure.

Of course, the main reason he's pressing me is that we are in heaven with our girl. May is a little song of joy, as she sleeps on our chests and crawls around after the cat. I would love to have another daughter, but I am dragging my feet.

China's one-child policy is still the law, and it applies to us as much as to a couple of farmers in the rice-fields of Hunan. To go back and adopt again we will have to state on all our application papers that we are childless.

I can't get excited about lying to the Chinese government. Isn't it wrong? — All my Quaker upbringing says that it is wrong! — and it seems risky as well. Don't they already have us on file? What happens if we arrive to adopt our girl and someone realizes our paperwork is a sham? Our adoption agency says it's fine, but I keep shaking my head, feeling heavy whenever Jack brings it up.

But he keeps pushing. "What is your *problem*?" he says. "The adoption agency has already brought back the first group of families with their second daughters. They didn't get in trouble."

On a hot June day, I go into our local library to ponder. The library is a tall sunlit space with high windows, giant stylized leaves on the ceiling and the smell of children and paper. I sit with my journal at a long wooden table, the low mumble of voices making it somehow easier to think. I write, look out the windows, write. And slowly the water inside me clears and I see the whole thing differently. My focus changes: instead of seeing the Chinese government, I see the baby.

Her life is what we're talking about here. The one-child policy appears suddenly in my mind as a curtain, a veil, not a substantial thing. I stop believing in it. The birth mother breaks the law by abandoning her, and I'm going to break the law by adopting her, but a law that forces the mother to leave her baby in a box in some public space is a wrong law. And it's a wrong law that would keep us from picking her up and bringing her home. I imagine that woman, sad and scared, handing the baby to me through the curtain.

***

Jenny, when we meet her, is solemn-eyed, bald as a bean, wearing a pink dress and tiny green jelly shoes. It is fourteen months since my come-to-Jesus day in the library, and she is fourteen months old. The middle-aged nanny who brings her to our hotel hallway proudly pinches her leg so we can see that she has been well fed. Jenny sobs and wails when she is handed to me and finally lunges from my arms into Jack's. He's proud to be chosen and rocks her, walks the halls with her. She howls for hours. The next day she attaches to me like a limpet, fiercely melting onto my chest as we ride the bus to our appointment with the provincial officials. They give us her little red passport and declare that she is officially ours. She does not let go for anything.

A month after we come home with our daughter, the Chinese government ends its one-child policy. That curtain was more tattered than I realized.

THE GIRLS

One of the themes of fairy tales is:

Be careful what you wish for.

I'd wished hard for over a decade to have children.

So how did that work out for me?

It worked out like a long waltz with a good partner, like sunlight on the skin, like warm bread and roses. I am there to marvel as these daughters grow into themselves, and that is a good thing for everyone.

They are in many ways opposite characters. May was evidently born knowing how to read. At four she writes poems and memorizes books. She makes up all the stories that the two girls act out. Jenny is her adoring minion. Reading comes slowly—she lives in her body. At two, she stares at ballet dancers on the TV, her eyes on the principal dancer, a man in red tights. "I be the pink one," she says, watching his every move. In preschool I sign her up for KinderDance. While the other little girls twirl around in their tutus, she is all focus, intent on the footwork.

Are they lucky to have landed here? To have been transplanted? Abandoned by some sad mother who wanted—needed—to have a son who would take care of her when she got old? Scooped out of their orphanages, scooped into a world so at odds with the crowded, tightly watched culture they would have grown up in?

Oliver, our sweet-natured guide in China, was sure they were lucky. While he shepherded us—six families with our new daughters—around to sign papers, visit doctors, see tourist sights, he told us how much he wanted to study in America.

"It's easier to get into heaven than it is to get into the United States," he told us.

To even apply for a visa he would have to quit his job and lose his apartment—and not get them back when the visa was declined, as it was likely to be. And here, without any effort on their part, these "lowest of the low" babies were being airlifted to America. He was jealous and open about it.

Sure, they're lucky. Maybe later they will feel some wound, some trauma from this crazy, cross-culture transplant—I don't know. For now, they are lucky to have each other, to grow up alongside someone with the same story. Lucky to have me as a mother because I watch them with such wonder. Lucky that Jack is willing to support us all. And lucky to grow up in a house where ducklings come in the mail.

After coming back from China with May, we move to a sort of pocket farm. I sell my rickety white house in Newberg to make the down payment on an old house with an acre and a half at the edge of Portland, along the Springwater Trail. It has hundred-year-old fir trees, long grass and a big shop. We plant fruit trees and giant pumpkins, raspberries, a huge garden. Jack builds chicken coops and a giant woodshed.

Animals start to appear. Swedish Blue and Rouen ducklings arrive in a flat cardboard box, two or three days old, sturdy and cheerful, gold and brown fluffs that the girls can hold in their hands. We pick up chicks and goslings at the feed store. We buy a couple of sheep from a local farmer, hoping they will eat the half acre of weeds.

Some of this is a bust. Geese are terrible, sharp-eyed, all beak. We sell them right away. The bantam rooster jumps on the hood of the station wagon when I drive up with the girls, staring in through the windshield, ready to attack. I keep a stick in the car to whack him away, a little black feathery football, while the girls race into the house. And the goddam sheep, with their voices like broken machinery! One day a stray dog chases them through the electric fence, and I have to hunt them down in the neighborhood. When I find one, I try to drag her home. She weighs as much as a couch and lies down in the gravel whenever a car goes by. Yikes. Where is a sheepdog when you need one? We return them to their farm.

But the red hens make good eggs and let me pet them, and the ducks are a joy. The girls name them after constellations: Orion, Cassiopeia. We dig a pond for them (and we welcome

visiting wild ducks). The girls play all summer on The Hill—
the dirt that came out of the pond.

It is beautiful, ragged, abundant chaos, our place, with always
too much to do, apples tumbling out of trees, wood to be
stacked and carried, seeds to plant and water and weed, girls
to rock and read to. I seize a practice of writing a poem every
morning, inspired by Bill Stafford's daily poems, so I catch
some moments of this chaos on the wing.

SNOWING

Why should I be surprised
that Jin May loves the stuff I love–
that at six she is wild for
The Lord of the Rings,
and presses her ear to the speaker
to hear an old-time hymn,
or Norman Blake playing
You Are My Sunshine on his banjo–
why am I startled
to have this tender, watchful child
soak up Shakespeare, or beg to make books
and collages, or chant long poems in the car?

It makes me cry– I did not know
that it would be this way. I put
the music on, I have the books around,
I live my life here, five feet up.
A couple of feet down
it's snowing, apparently– the girls
are sticking out their tongues to catch
the flakes, soft and cold, of what
nourishes me, and I see through tears
that it feeds them too.

TIME FOR SCHOOL

1999

A public school with a Chinese immersion program is starting up a few miles from us. Perfect! Kindergarten will have English classes in the morning and Chinese in the afternoon. We sign May up, but I think it will be a shock to go from playing at home to going to school all day. So, when she is four, I set out to find a preschool she can attend a few mornings a week. A place to get used to the idea of school.

I have a list. "Beauty and order" is at the top of it. Kindness. Nature. Not too far from our house, etc. It's fun, visiting schools. I'm fascinated by how people create a space for children. But none of the places I visit seems right.

Finally I visit the Franciscan Montessori Earth School. It goes up through 8th grade, and is a pretty big school.. Though it's quite nearby, I haven't checked it out before because I don't want her to have to go every single morning, which they require. Still, it's so close; I should at least see it.

I get to the school for my appointment with Sister Kathleen Ann, one of the Franciscan nuns who run the school. On the glass front door is a sign:

Reception with Terry Tempest Williams, 3 pm.

I feel an odd punch of surprise. Terry Tempest Williams — a famous, wonderful nature writer — is *here*? On the gritty outer edge of southeast Portland? What kind of school is this, that wants her — and can get her?

I push open the glass doors and there in the hall is someone I know! Priscilla, a quiet, precise teacher, took a bookbinding class with me a few years ago. We hug and laugh.

Sister Kathleen Ann is stout and square, with intelligent eyes and the force of a breaking wave. I ask her about Terry Tempest Williams. "She's here as part of our nature writing program. It's the EARTH school," she says with a grin. I'm still shaking my head. Then she tours me around the classrooms.

The children are busy—and calm. They trace sandpaper letters on the floor, pour water into pitchers, carefully wipe off tables. Everything—the racks of colored beads, the rocking chair, the shelves of books—looks enticing. I'm smitten. Beauty and order in spades.

We enroll May, knowing she will go to Chinese school next year. She gets my bookbinding student Priscilla as her teacher. And it's so lovely that we throw Chinese school out the window (a fork in the road)—and send Jenny along next fall, to join her in Priscilla's Children's House class—the class for four-, five-, and six year-olds.

The nature writer thing continues to be an amazement. Each year the nuns host a dinner for the visiting writer, at the Italian villa in the Columbia Gorge where they live. I get to have dinner with some of my heroes: Barry Lopez, Peter Matthiessen, Pattiann Rogers.

This is extraordinary, but it's only one way in which I feel the resonance of this place with my own young dreams of starting a school. There are deep spiritual roots here: peace, simplicity, earth stewardship, community. Quaker values that turn out to also be Franciscan. Maria Montessori had peace in mind when she developed her pedagogy: "Establishing lasting peace is the work of education; all politics can do is keep us out of war."

I love to stand next to Mother Francine, the slender white-haired flame of life who started the school, when we drop the girls off every morning. Her presence and grace warm the hallway. She knows every child—all 230 of them. She knows me. My respect for her fills me like a well.

I have no idea, as I stand beside her watching children flow past, that this school is a field in which we will wander—as students, as parents, as teachers—for the next twenty years.

And yet—amidst all this joy, I am unhappy.

TROUBLE

At this time I belong to a little Quaker women's group called Multwood. We are doing our bit to mend the long-time schism between Meeting and Church Quakers. We have potlucks, read books, wrestle with our differing theologies. In June 2000, we all agree to read the book *Love Is Stronger than Death* over the summer break, and talk about it when we meet again in the fall.

The book is the true, gritty love story of two aging, profoundly spiritual people: Rafe, a Trappist monk, and a priest, Cynthia Bourgeault, who authored the book. Rafe knows he is dying and prepares Cynthia to carry on their love affair past his death.

Reading this story triggers in me a rough despair. Rafe and Cynthia's love is the kind of love that I recognize I was made for—honest, spiritually raw, full of the power to heal. But it's as far from my own marriage as the Grand Canyon is from the moon. Jack isn't spiritual, he's a practical businessman. I knew that all along. He has changed, though. Since his mother died, not long after Jenny came to us, all his old alcohol-fumed wounds seem to focus on me. Where he used to be mostly playful and cheerful, with the occasional spasm of fury, now he is mostly grim and harsh, with the odd moment of good cheer. He looks at my spiritual activities with bitter suspicion. Still, I have chosen a life with him, and we have these marvelous daughters. I will not give up. I already divorced once; I'm not going to fail again. I'm going to do the right thing. Make up for how my dad did it, make up for how unreliable I used to be.

This book is like a lamp, showing me what I long for and how far, how infinitely far, I am from it. But I don't see a thing to do. At this point I can no more access the sense of agency and awe of the sheetrock moment in the *Isn't the Mind Amazing?* dream than I can pick up my car.

Out of this despair arises a strange dream.

June 2000
46 years old

I'm with a small group of Quakers. We are reading the book *Love Is Stronger than Death*. Something in the book makes me aware that I am in big trouble—that an alien presence has taken up residence in my head. It's a predator of some kind. Once I know it's there, I can feel the deadening, flattening weight of it. I suspect it has been in there for years. I feel hopeless, now that I have noticed it. I pound my forehead on the floor in despair.

Then I sit up. Here are all these spiritual people. Could I get these Quakers to pray it out of me? I start to explain my problem, but I'm inarticulate and slow. I feel guilty for taking up so much time. I tell about the predator but only get to my prayer idea at the very end.

We go out on a lawn to set up the ritual. What a relief. It's finally going to happen.

But the automatic sprinklers go on, watering the place where the ritual was to take place. We go back in. I'm disappointed but resigned: *Well, maybe tomorrow. I've lived with this a very long time, I guess I can stand it another day or so.*

This dream leaves me with a dry, sickening sense of fear. Now that it's been named, I recognize a deadening energy in my mind. Just as in the dream, I'm terrified, in a kind of enduring way. I carry this dread all through the summer, a shadow over my busy life. I can't wait to tell the dream to the women in Multwood. I think they must be the group of Quakers that the dream suggests could offer help, could pray the thing out of my head. Finally we meet again for our fall potluck. After dinner I jump into the conversation and tell my dream.

But nothing happens! They hum and cough, pass the brownies, and talk about something else.

As I drive the hour home on the dark freeway, my chest is heavy. It's the same dull hopelessness I felt at the end of the dream: *Well, I've lived with this a long time; I guess I can wait a little longer.*

A question . . .

Before we get to the next bit of the story, we need to look at what I thought was happening. Did I really believe I was occupied by an alien force? That a predator had taken up residence in my mind?

Or did I think it was a symbolic message, in the usual way of dreams?

Well, both, really. It was a scary and visceral dream, and it woke me up to the fact that something was definitely wrong. I took it at face value, while also recognizing it as a symbolic story. I had been a woman with a great sense of agency over her life, and now I was steadily falling into a black hole of powerlessness. How did that happen?

In *The Four-Gated City*, Doris Lessing writes about the self-hater, an inner voice that undermines us, echoing all the critical things anyone has ever said to us. It works hard to keep us down. I think of the predator in my dream as something like that. I'd allowed Jack's criticism and anger to cohabitate with my guilt over being too flighty in my youth. I didn't fight back with my own anger, or my own sturdiness—I collapsed, for the sake of having children and an image of myself as a decent person. This fear–guilt combo took over my operating system. It was like a virus; I let it get the upper hand. The dream's term "predator" did seem symbolic, but I also physically *felt* the pressure and presence of this frozen energy, once it had been called out. And I had no clue what to do about it except to follow the dream's suggestion of getting some spiritual people to pray it out of there. So I was very disappointed when my dream-telling at the potluck fell with such a dull thud.

However, it wasn't as dull a thud as I thought. Someone had heard what I couldn't quite bring myself to say.

A couple of weeks after the meeting, Peggy, a minister from the Church side of the Quaker aisle, calls me.

"Tina. I wonder if we missed something. Were you asking for prayers?"

"Yes, oh, I really was."

"Well, Alivia and I have some experience in this kind of thing. Shall we come up and see you?"

"Would you? That would be wonderful."

It's a clear October day when Peggy and Alivia roar up the driveway on their big motorcycles. They park under the fir trees in front of our house. Peggy is tall, bright, and angular; Alivia quiet and round, a dove. They dump their helmets and jackets on the porch and come inside to sit on the purple futon. We chat a few minutes, and then they ask me to retell the dream. They've heard it once before, at the meeting three weeks ago. Outside, a coyote comes to stand in the driveway, his fur fluffy in the sunlight. I point him out. Peggy and Alivia shake their heads at the way the dream seems to have seeped into the daylight world. A big predator, hmm.

I can't get over the fact that they are here. The relief of seeing them drive up. My amazement that they want to help me. I am not in a doubting frame of mind; I trust that this is what the dream prescribed. I truly hate the feeling of this deadening, flattening force. If this is the way to deal with it, let's go.

The coyote stands in the driveway, eyeing the ducks. I sit in a wooden chair by the woodstove. Alivia puts her hands on my shoulders, acting as a channel for the light. Peggy holds my hands, to be the drain for whatever might come out. We sit for a few minutes. I can sense them praying, though we are silent and my eyes are closed. Then I feel a heavy rush of chilly energy run through my body, almost nauseating. I shiver and open my eyes.

We are quiet for a minute, and Peggy describes what she felt.

"It was a blue-green swirl of energy." She moves her hands to show how big, and how it moved. "These things can be more like illness, or like darkness. That was definitely on the *dark* end."

I feel soft, raw, edgeless, as we sit together on the couch. They tuck a blanket around me and cuddle up right close, since I am chattering with cold. Then they feed me toast and cream cheese, and when they drive away, I go off to school to pick up the girls, quieter inside than I've felt in years.

That Peggy heard my unvoiced request and called me and *knew what to do;* I'm grateful for that to this day. I truly felt helped by their intervention. It was very odd, I know. If I hadn't had their prayers, maybe I could have dealt with my "predator" some other way. If I was lucky, a really good therapist. Not that Jack would have paid for that. Something, I'm sure, would have eventually broken my trance of endurance—a car accident, or a breakdown of some kind. But in fact, this is the help I got. Symbolic all the way, but literal, too. You could see it as an enactment, like a play—but just as with a play, the more you participate in its internal reality, the greater the catharsis.

As I look back at my story, this seems like the moment when my toes touched the bottom of the stream I was drowning in, and I pushed off toward the surface. I wasn't "cured" by a long shot—I had years of work ahead to rebuild my life on different terms. It was a beginning, however: the first step of coming home to myself.

POEMS

I'm in the kitchen on the phone, staring out at our two grumpy sheep and tangles of blackberries under the big fir trees. The peeling yellow linoleum is patched with strapping tape, dishes are piled in the sink. On the phone is my friend Polly in Canada, my long-legged poet roommate from Argenta, twenty years ago.

"I should write more poems," she says.

"Me too. You know, Bill Stafford wrote a poem every morning. Maybe we could try that."

"Okay. We could mail them to each other once a week."

As lightly as that, the practice of writing a daily poem sails into my life. Every Monday we mail seven poems to each other. In envelopes, with stamps.

Polly stops after about six months, but two years later I am still at it, driven by a hunger to touch down—even for fifteen minutes a day—inside my experience. These poems, this practice, turns on an engine inside me. I become alert for poems. I start to pay attention. I see poems as I watch the girls dig on the Hill and build imaginary fires during a hailstorm. I start to take in the smell of my life, in all of its sacred mess. This changes everything.

HAWKEYE

Hold on.
Is she in danger? Is there more we should be doing?

She's going to be all right.
She listened to the Predator dream.
She has the children she longed for.
She's milking the cow, with her daily poem practice.

We can't make her see, but we can water the seeds of her seeing.

If only she would realize her power!

SIX
In which I acquire a magical tool

WITTA — *Dream*

January 10, 2001
47 years old

I'm in a big building in a faraway place.

Someone tells me about a being called the Witta.

"There's one in every generation. You can tell who it is because they can float up."

Well, I can float up, I think to myself, *so there must be more to it than that.*

The Witta scares people somehow; its power disturbs them.

I'm in my hotel room. A boorish man tries to get into bed with me and I don't want him there. He gets out, and then hassles me by rolling golf balls around on the desk, making a big racket. I get up to look for someone to help me get rid of him. But people are stirring, so I get up and begin to get ready too.

We go into a huge open space like a giant train station. I scan the crowd, still looking for help. Lots of people are headed somewhere, all going to the same place. Dark, dim colors, anxious people. I see a few familiar faces. But soon they're gone, and I'm left walking through a crowd of strangers who look back at me without recognition or interest.

I can't stand it. Then several things happen at once. I allow myself to know that I am in fact the Witta, and my body explodes with energy. I stamp my foot and shoot up into the rafters: I realize it, reveal it, and release it in the same fiery, heart-pounding moment. The crowd panics.

I hover in the dome, watching people scramble out, until finally there are only five or six people left, sitting on the floor in red and white striped suits. I love them for not running away. I float down and sit with them.

They are prisoners. Their striped suits are prison uniforms. Manacles around their ankles go down into the floor. Their guard ran off in the general panic, but they couldn't run. They are not afraid at all. I tell them of my gratitude and love. They have bandanas around their heads, with the design upside down.

"Why are you wearing your bandanas backwards?" I ask.

"It's like politics," one woman says. "Anything is possible in a world where bandanas are on backwards."

I wake up from this dream feeling sick. That surge of anger and energy and revelation when I admit I am the Witta has left me ill. I keep shuddering. The unbearableness of those empty eyes! The roar of intensity when I admit who I am!

This dream terrifies me.

I *do* want to be seen, known. I can't stand to be looked at with empty eyes. But I do not want to be *that* kind of special — the kind that makes you run away.

I learned early on that I could get something that looked a lot like love by being helpful. I learned to guess what my parents wanted and jump to meet their needs before they even asked. I ran my life on that program until I married Jack. Now my jumpiness leads only to more work. Not love. I can scurry to help and please and appease him all day every day, and he still won't recognize what kind of creature he lives with. And he'll descend into a chilly rage if I cook the wrong thing or fail to pull the hairs off my upper lip.

It has begun to dawn: No one will understand me if I don't. No one will see me as powerful unless I do. No one will recognize me if I don't recognize myself. No one can free me except me.

I'm good at feeling grief, raw endurance, overwhelm, longing. Anger, no. Jack gets mad at me; I don't get mad at him. I cringe and shrink. Fear of my husband's bitter voice has frozen me. I am the prisoners tied to the floor in this dream.

What the prisoners say with their bandanas is crucial. They have a sense of infinite possibility. They are the opposite of all those dim, anxious people in the train station — the anxious, dim, muddled parts of my energy, the parts that can't imagine anything different or new.

The revelation of my strange power, and my feeling of love for the prisoners, and their message that *anything is possible* clears out the room. I'm on the cusp of change after this dream.

I have a life-saving conversation around this time with my

spiritual director, Bill. We sit together in his office, surrounded by pieces of his blown-glass art. I've been seeing him for a few months, once a month. On this day he talks about the wisdom of desire.

"You know what?" he says. "Every day I write down ten things I want. I write each desire on a three-by-five card, and I keep them in a card file."

"What kind of things?"

"All sorts of things. A hot tub for our back deck. A trip to the Grand Canyon. To be wide awake. To make more time for my art.

"But," he says, "the key is that you separate the desire from any expectation of getting it. This is not about what you think you can have, but what you allow yourself to want."

Doesn't he sound like the bird-girl from the *Ask for Horses* dream? Ask, ask, ask more bravely! Don't settle for what has been laid out for you.

Then he says, "I get up at 5:30 to do this, and so does my wife. Then we share our cards. It is a royal road to intimacy."

My heart hurts. It's the same feeling I had after reading *Love Is Stronger than Death*. This is what a relationship *might* be like—deep, courageous wondering and talking, companioning each other on a spiritual adventure. Damn, it's a far cry from the marriage I am in. My chest feels heavy and cold. What is going to happen to me? I can't imagine leaving Jack. What about the girls? What about my commitment?

But this dream, after I recover from the shock of it, stiffens my spine. Anything is possible in a world where bandanas are on upside down.

Or in which I write down, every morning, ten things I want.

HAWKEYE

All right! We have her attention.

TRIP TO BERKELEY

October 2001
48 years old

My friend Elizabeth stops me in the lobby of the Earth School one afternoon and says, "Do you want to go to Berkeley?"

"Always," I say.

"Well, the Dalai Lama's doctor is going to be there next month. Maybe he can help me with my multiple sclerosis. If I buy your ticket, will you come along and take notes so I can concentrate on what he's saying?"

A month later, on a futon couch in a bungalow in Berkeley, I chat with a cheerful young man in a green shirt and his smiley wife, who are also waiting their turn to see Yeshi Dhonden. I mention a dream I had that morning and they lean forward.

"Do you know Jeremy Taylor?" the man says.

"No."

"Wow, well you should totally look him up. He teaches here in Oakland. He is an amazing teacher of dreamwork."

His wife pulls out a copy of Jeremy's book *Where People Fly and Water Runs Uphill.* Their enthusiasm doubles the light in the room.

A few minutes later we are called in to see Dr. Dhonden, who is the most grounded human being ever to cross my path. With his dark hooded eyes and polished skull, he seems to have grown out of the earth. He feels Elizabeth's pulse, looks at her tongue, smells the urine sample she brought, and says, through a translator, that she has an "imbalance in her life-sustaining wind." He prescribes some herbs and some changes to her diet. As we leave the room, I feel like we've stepped from Berkeley through a portal into a cave somewhere—Tibet, I guess—and talked with a 200-year-old turtle. Not your typical trip to the doctor.

Elizabeth stays with Dr. Dhonden's protocol for a few months and then gives it up. It doesn't click with her. But I buy the book *Where People Fly and Water Runs Uphill,* and it lifts me like a sail in the wind. It tells how to start and run a dream group. Six of my friends and I start to meet once a month in my living room to share our dreams and work on them. I make soup, they bring bread and chocolate.

I've been writing down my dreams for a long time, but that futon couch in Berkeley is a threshold to a new phase. With the start of my dream group, I become part of a tribe, instead of a solo traveler in dreamland. We know so much about the underground currents in each other's lives. How precious it is to be known, and to know each other in this way!

That Yeshi Dhonden, with his taproot to the center of the world, is in the next room when the young couple tells me about Jeremy—that does not hurt the magic at all.

July 2002
49 years old

I'm standing on a cliff with my brother-in-law Tim. We are looking out over the river, talking about how you make change in the world.

I say, "It just takes two things. First, you sit still. Then, you figure out what you love. After you've done that, you can do anything. You can take down a dam."

"No," he says, shaking his head.

"Yes, it's true."

I see the huge dam, like the Dalles Dam, and near it a tiny human being.

"Because," I tell him, "the person is *alive*, and the dam is dead."

I can *see* it, looking at the barely visible person way down there. Size is nothing; aliveness is all.

HOW YOU MAKE CHANGE IN THE WORLD
— Reflection

This is surely a political dream, helping me with my life-long inquiry about social change, but it is not only political. Dreams are amazing in their ability to cram many levels of meaning into a single image. "Overdetermined" was Jeremy Taylor's word for this. They collect messages about creativity, spiritual issues, physical health, sexuality, practical matters, and the state of the planet into one symbolic story, which is why they can be read on so many levels. So when this dream shows an image of the big industrial dam, it's also talking about my life.

The prisoners in the *Witta* dream also make the link between social action and personal recovery. "It's like politics: anything is possible in a world where bandanas are upside down." This is paradoxical, since bandanas have symmetrical designs—in some way, bandanas are *always* on upside down.

These dreams both say: don't focus on how hopeless it all seems or how small you feel up against the status quo. That doesn't matter. And it is not action that begins the work of change. The first step is the opposite of taking action.

Sit still.

Aliveness is all.

Discover what you love.

These recent dreams—*Predator, Witta,* and *How You Make Change in the World*—portray blocked energy. A deadening force, a predator, occupies my head. I pretend I am helpless, when in fact I am scarily powerful. I face a giant industrial dam.

But the dreams will not let me get away with staying stuck. They give me clues:

How to get rid of the predator.

The raw experience of my power.

The phrase "Anything is possible."

The flame of aliveness of a person, so different from the deadness of the dam.

The dreams want me to come unstuck, and they are eerily

patient with me. They seem to know that becoming friends with my power will be the work of years.

It will help to sit still, get quiet, access the living stream of what I love.

But at this moment that seems as distant and unlikely as the tiny person bringing down a dam.

I've made a list of everything I'm doing. It fills six pages. It is horrible. Looking at it I feel so inadequate and lonely, a ragged mess. All my time is spent scrambling to take care of the next thing. The only time I sit still is the moment I take at the kitchen table to scribble my poem every morning, a moment both beautiful and starved.

MAGICAL TOOLS — *Dream*

May 22, 2003
49 years old

A long, involved dream in two parts.

Part I:
I am trying to go home, back to my mother's house. I do this periodically but unconsciously. Suddenly I think, *I don't want to go through this routine anymore. Why am I doing it, anyway?*

I go back into the house which I share with Jack and other people. I ask Mr. Scott, the drama teacher, why I keep doing this, and he says, "Because you don't own your own house anymore. You used to, but now you rent. You go back to visit your mom because you want to be *in the presence of ownership.*"

I get it.

He adds, looking at me intently, "You're not using your creativity enough. Taking a couple of classes would probably do it."

I think, *Yes!*

Part II:
I'm walking along a bridge on a big road, several lanes of heavy traffic going both ways. An accident up ahead: a child has been hit, and is being dragged, smashed. Cars swerve and slam into each other. The mother screams, races through the traffic to lie over the child and cry. I don't want to go over to them—it's too awful—but I still want to help, so I run toward the traffic and wave my arms to try to slow the cars down. No one pays any attention. At first there are cars, but soon I'm waving at ranks of dusty overcrowded buses with people hanging off the sides, and then walking through crowds of people on the sidewalk, in fairy-tale Mideastern costumes: bright colors, turbans, women in red boxes. Finally, I end up alone in an open

outdoor corridor, like a monastery walkway, it's getting dark, and the flavor of the dream gets deeper, more numinous.

An Arab magician on the balcony above the walkway is assembling power, gathering power out of the air and summoning magical tools. One of the tools he summons comes to me, chooses me instead.

It is a bell-shaped heavy object of solid blown glass—golden brown with white speckles like a cowrie shell. It fits warmly in my hand and is awake, *alive*, intelligent, intensely beautiful, and conscious. Having it enables me to understand something, or to move differently, to glide. The man gets onto a large golden blown-glass apple and rides it down off the balcony and out of the courtyard. I get another object of power but don't recall what it is.

This dream has several stories in it. The first one concerns my acupuncturist, a round-faced, self-assured man named Gonzo. I start seeing him for back pain, but he takes on a bigger job—trying to release my dammed-up energy, my stuck *qi*. He studied *curanderismo,* shamanism, with his Mexican grandmother and is not your garden-variety acupuncturist.

I have this dream at the beach, during a camping trip with my daughter's third-grade class. A week later, I am on my way to see Gonzo, driving along the freeway thinking about the magical tool. The weight and the *consciousness* of it are still vivid, as real in my hand as the steering wheel. It doesn't seem like a symbol; more like an actual thing. But what?

When I get to my session, Gonzo looks at my tongue and takes hold of my wrist. "You know," he says while he listens to my pulse, "recently in my meditation I was working with your energy. I was recalibrating it. It looked like a Radio Shack had exploded in your back. And you were trying to acquire some magical tools."

"Magical tools!" I stare at him. "I just got some! *How did you know?*"

This is very odd. I've never even heard the term before I heard it in the dream.

I describe the heavy, wide-awake glass being. "I've been wondering what it could be."

"I know what it is."

He is casual. "Have you seen stars in it? Stars shining out of it?"

"No . . . though it has white speckles."

"Well, next time you see it, look for stars."

"What is it?"

"It's your own universe. Your own way of seeing things. In another time, you would have been one of those people who could get it to snow."

He tells me about my other tool, the one I couldn't quite see in the dream. "It looks like half of a cut-open pepper."

Later he asks, "What have you done with your magical tools so far?"

"Nothing! I only got them last Thursday," I say, still rattled by his prescience, and amused at how normal he makes it all sound.

But after I leave his office I start to think about the morning I woke up from the dream, a sunny day by the ocean. Three unusual things happened that morning, and I wonder if they are somehow related to the dream.

As soon as I ducked out of my tent in the morning I started to shape sand into a big spiral. Kids sat down to watch. I patted and scooped, happy, building, making. When the spiral got so big it had to pass through an outcropping of black rock, suddenly it had an edge to it, a wilder energy.

Later in the morning, I taught the kids a guest lesson about deep time. I asked them to stand in a line on the beach holding a long string, each child representing a generation. We talked about grandparents, great-great-grandparents, ancestors. This was a rare blast of teaching something straight from my soul. I wanted them to feel they were part of a stream: not lonely critters who'd been plopped down here like aliens but recipients of a great heritage of endurance and intelligence. I hoped to kindle a little awe and maybe gratitude.

Finally, a tall man came running down onto the beach just before lunch. His son was on the camping trip; he was late. I ran up to greet him, and we started to laugh. Fifteen years later, René is one of my dearest friends. We are still laughing.

So, who knows? Are these the ordinary-but-wonderful things that happen when I am in touch with *my own way of seeing*? There's nothing "magical" about any of that, and yet, in retrospect, there was an unusual surge of life and creativity in me that morning.

But there is a lot more to this dream than the magical tool.

It shows me waking up to a wrong situation, one I've been asleep in. I don't own my home, my sense of sovereignty. The remedy for this is to ignite my creativity. This is not the first or the last time the dream-makers suggest that.

The dream also shows how unwilling I am to face my pain: I can't bear to go over and comfort the mother with the crushed child.

But the thing I *can* do—run upstream, against the flow of traffic (as in the *Weather Underground* dream)—leads me through layers of meaning, through increasingly flavorful, colorful buses and people, right up into the dream dimension, where something astonishing shows up to help me.

This heavy glass object, *my own universe,* is a being of some kind, a living consciousness. If I learn how to work with it, the dream says—and I believe—it will help me take ownership of my life. Which has been my task ever since the *Predator* dream showed me how completely I had lost my way.

CELL IN THE GREAT BEING – *Revelation*

August 15, 2003
49 years old

Dark middle of the night, Jack and the girls asleep around me. I am awake, following a rabbit hole which has led me down the compelling but ungraspable matter of *scale*. I am trying to fit five million red blood cells into a point of blood the size of a period, while also imagining that our galaxy — in which our planet is a dust mote — has billions of sister galaxies. I can't get my mind around it, but I feel weirdly opened up. Then, right there in the dark, great invisible arms wrap around me.

This comes with a full-body realization: *I am a cell in some great being*.

I understand that I am to this vast being exactly as one of my cells is to me: an essential, conscious, mortal particle. What is more, this being (Earth?) is wide awake. It is far more aware and conscious than I am, just as I am, I believe, more conscious than my cells. I know that my cells are intelligent, complex, and community-minded, but I also imagine that I grasp a bigger picture than they do. The same is true of the great being, only now *I'm* the cell with a limited view. I'm part of Someone or Something that understands itself through my eyes, through my liveliness — and not just mine, but clams and dirt and hummingbirds and bristlecone pines. Our life is its life. The whole thing is an intimacy of existence that is stranger than we can think, but for a moment I feel it, get it, expand into it. The question of scale was too much for my mind, so some other part of me took over and let me *know* it.

For a couple of weeks after this night I float on a stream of relief. I accept my own death with a new tenderness: when I go, the great being will continue. I am part of it, instead of "me." My body is made of particles of joy.

*Such encounters with the outrageous scale of the larger
Body we inhabit bring a shuddering humility, yet they
can also release an unexpected intuition of safety, a sense
of being held and sustained by powers far larger than
anything we can comprehend.*

— David Abram, *Becoming Animal*

Gonzo is partly responsible for this revelation as well.

After about a year of working with him, he feels my pulse one afternoon and says, "You're much better. Your stress is less. But you still have this sense of impending doom."

I laugh. "You can tell that from my pulse? But you're right. What can I do about that?"

He looks at me sternly. "If you're really serious, you can do this meditation. Every day for half an hour, sit and imagine a stream of gold light as wide as your hips going down to the center of the Earth. If you do this for six months you should feel a shift."

It is not that easy to envision a beam of light 4,000 miles long, going down from my hips through the floor, the dirt, the tectonic plates, all the way to the molten core. I keep at it, though can only manage about fifteen minutes a day. Still, the shift happens much faster than he said it would. It is only a couple of months before that awakening in the dark. I'm sure that practice helped to plug me into the connection with the great being. And my sense of impending doom is gone like dew under sunlight.

A BOOK

I've self-published three poetry chapbooks, one each November for three years, culled from the torrent of daily poems. But in the fourth year, I have no book for the family craft sale on the day after Thanksgiving. Maybe I could try prose? Could I trace the threads of hunger and dream, the crooked byways that had led me to that moment of being embraced in the dark, the moment when I felt the great being?

> *I gained it so by climbing slow*
> *By clutching at the twigs that grow*
> *Between the bliss and me . . .*
>   —Emily Dickinson

I scramble for three months and it comes into being: a fifty-page book, *Asking for Horses*, self-published, ready just in time. It's lovely. I reveal so much, freely drawing the picture of my overwhelmed life, my earnest spiritual seeking. I talk about the poetry practice and Gonzo. I bring in dreams: *Witta, Predator, Magical Tools*. The culmination is that moment of belonging, when the great being wrapped her arms around me. The book is honest and soft, self-aware, but to go through it now, reading between the lines, makes me grimace a little because of what I did not admit.

My husband reads it before the craft sale.

"Why would anyone want to read this?" he asks.

This is like the moment in the *Witta* dream, in the gray train station. Here is my old terror of not being seen, of being looked at with empty eyes.

He might have been fretting about his image. I do mention the fights we are having about the roof. He's decided to re-roof our old house, and I resent having to spend hours up there yanking off shingles, stretched as I am. But mostly I am generous to him in the book. I hold out a hopeful note for our marriage.

Dreams layer on themselves, come true in various ways over time . . .

By writing and publishing this book I give life to the moment in the *Witta* dream when I shoot up off the floor. The urge to be known fuels my telling. I reveal myself to myself at the same time I reveal it to the world. By publishing it, I say: "This is who I am. If it scares you, too bad." And the dam breaks. *One day* after the craft sale, I see what I've been refusing to see: I am scared of my husband. I am miserable in my marriage.

The next couple of weeks are grim. Now that I know I have to say something, I feel hot, scared, determined. To make it worse, I run across a book while Christmas shopping: *Why Does He Do That?: Inside the Minds of Angry and Controlling Men.* Lundy Bancroft, the author, runs treatment programs for abusive men. I hide this book when I'm not reading it. It dawns on me how much I have shrunk to avoid Jack's anger, though he is not physically violent.

My adrenaline and fear mount by the day. I have to do something. I decide to get a babysitter and take Jack out on New Year's for a conversation. But Christmas morning comes. He will not get out of bed. The girls, eight and six years old, are sitting under the tree surrounded by gifts, ready; the candles are lit. We wait. He doesn't get up. After a few hours of stalling, my heart breaking for the girls, I go in and sit on the bed next to him. I say, "This is unacceptable. So much about this marriage is unacceptable. If you don't see a counselor with me, I'm out of here with the girls."

HAWKEYE

Beautiful, beautiful!
Right into the arms of the Great Being.
"A drop in the ocean wakes up and realizes the whole ocean is awake."
It's moving at last.

We have Gonzo to thank. He's tuned right in to the likes of us; we couldn't have done it without him.

She's not out of the woods, though.
No.
It's going to be a thornbush to get out of this marriage.
Oh goodness yes.

For one thing, she cannot roar.
Quakerism, which gave her so much—the presence of strong women, a love of silence, the awareness of God in everyone— also crippled her. It told her to be quiet.

.

SEVEN

In which I dig up the buried treasure

BYRON KATIE

February 2004

A short white-haired woman walks up the aisle toward the front of the Unity Church. People stand and clap. She looks too small for all this clapping. For the next couple of hours, however, as Byron Katie invites people onto the stage, asking questions and telling stories, the bottom slowly falls out of my world. I want to be her. I want to stand *there*, where she stands, on planet freedom.

One of the women who comes up to talk with her believes a childhood trauma has left her mentally ill. Another is a doctor, afraid she has contracted a fatal illness from a patient. A third woman is scared about money and thinks she might end up homeless with her son. Katie calls them honey, and asks questions. *Is it true? What happens when you believe that thought? Who would you be if you didn't believe it?*

I'd read Katie's book *Loving What Is* a year before, but I didn't get it until I saw her in person. She really seems to be from another planet. The women who come up on stage are afraid—with good reason, it seems to me—of mental illness, death, homelessness. But Katie won't collaborate with their fear. Death doesn't frighten her, nor anything else. I watch each person's energy shift and relax under the light of her amusement and clarity.

I am at the church with Jack and two friends. They are impressed, but I am smitten.

I've caught a whiff of some living air that I need as much as food. It's not about the marriage; I still want to see a couples counselor with Jack, and he's agreed to go, but this is hunger from deeper territory.

"I want to go to the School for the Work," I tell Jack on the drive home.

That is Katie's nine-day intensive program in LA in November. He doesn't say no, but he won't pay for it. And I don't have $4000. I don't even have $400.

I do own something valuable, though: forty old books. The books I bought from George, the exquisite volumes that ignited the *Stars and Drop of Water* dream.

I load them into my car, and the girls and I drive west through hazelnut orchards to the hidden home of a rare book dealer. He comes out of his house—friendly, alert—and lays the books out on a picnic table. Most of them he hands back, but ten he wants to buy, and offers $5000 for. The girls sit in the car while he takes me in to get my check. He shows me around his collection, in a tall light room that could be in London or Rome. White-gloved assistants glance at me and smile. He pulls out drawers full of manuscripts that would make a monk weep. The place is walled with hundreds of leather-bound volumes, each as fine as the few he bought from me. It is like walking through a portal of filbert trees and finding myself in Oz. The books I bought from George ten years earlier have admitted me to this surprising place, a kind of book-lover's paradise. And as they leave me for paradise, they admit me to Byron Katie's School.

The School is a nonstop unraveling of my ordinary reality. We set out to make friends with the worst that can happen; we question things I didn't know were up for question. Laughing, dancing. So many bricks of my worldview are rearranged. One day, undone with gratitude, I go up to Katie and catch her on the stage before she leaves for lunch.

"I just want to thank you," I tell her.

"Oh," she says, holding my hands and looking in my eyes. "Angel mommy—mommy of the heart—*we've done our time*." She hugs me.

I cry and cry. Mommy of the heart!

I come home from the School full of tenderness for Jack. I've seen my part in the game—how I crave his love and approval and contort myself to get it. It's not his fault I make myself small. That's on me. I take responsibility for my nonsense. After nine days with Katie I know how to ask myself the questions she'd asked the women on stage at the Unity Church. I know my body's signals for a stressful belief, the way I scrinch my shoulders and hold my breath. I know how to unfold into a quieter, sweeter, don't-know space.

"Have the Work for breakfast," Katie tells us as we leave the School. And I do. Every morning. I've found a way to get relief without Jack having to change.

He thinks that's great. He's off the hook.

I am on fire. I teach workshops on Katie's Work at Portland Community College, hold a weekly drop-in group and see a few private clients. I lead a big workshop called "Activism from a Place of Peace," where I offer the Work to Quaker and Unitarian activists. Finally, I've found a way to be of genuine service.

Four months after I come home from the School, I have a dream.

KNIGHTS ERRANT — *Dream*

March 26, 2005
51 years old

A famous musician, like Bob Dylan, has died. His daughter is twelve years old, and she should have been rich, but the money vanished. Someone, maybe a trustee, has made off with it. No one knows what happened.

In the next scene, a man keeps grabbing at me. I can fly but he reaches and pulls me back down. He's not scary, but dorky, with big hair and a round face. Finally, I turn and look at him.

"What are you doing?"

He says: "I like you. We like each other."

I realize this is true. I stop resisting him. We are old friends, or will be.

Now that we are not fighting, we wonder what to do. We both like to solve problems, and an idea strikes us at the same time: we'll find out what happened to the girl's money!

We sail off to do that, like knights errant, with a high, eager energy. We enter a room where we think the evidence might be, and are brought up short. It is crammed to the ceiling with boxes: reams and reams of financial reports and records. This theft was committed in a complex, sophisticated way—like the Enron scandal—and it's not going to be solved with eagerness but with patience. It will take a *different kind of intelligence,* according to the dream. We come out of the room and take a deep breath, slowing down and preparing ourselves to go back in and study thousands of pieces of paper looking for the small deceptions.

This dream has an unmissable message: SLOW DOWN.

The problem is not my strength of intention. That's strong. The problem lies in my pace, my rush. Back up, it says: take a deep breath. Plan on years, miles, *reams* of work.

Let's say I'm the girl whose resources mysteriously disappeared. Those resources—courage, confidence, power—did not vanish in a single nasty instance of trauma but by way of thousands of small self-deceptions. I'd fallen into the quicksand of common beliefs: *Death is bad. I have to be careful. They'll reject me if I get too big. I have to get it right*...and on and on and on.

The persistence of these thoughts makes them seem like reality, even though they are only stories about reality. It will take commitment, patience, and glory—and years of practice—to move those stories out of my body.

I love the dream's message that my buddy and I are not giving up, just pacing ourselves for the long haul. I love, too, my sense that the guy who keeps grabbing at me is some version of my old round-faced enemy, the Moon Man. I finally turn around to face him and he becomes an ally. This is such a good sign.

Between the poetry practice, two years of spiritual direction training with the nuns in Mount Angel, my dream group, the *Predator* healing, the cell in the Great Being awakening, and the small book that arose from that, plus Katie's beautiful Work, life is pulsing up through the weight of my stone. It's possible that the *Stars and Drop of Water* dream of ten years ago, which told me that the purpose of an enemy can be to strengthen you, knew all about this crisis with Jack—and how it has made me rally my forces.

In visible ways, I am stepping into bigger shoes. I serve three years as clerk of my Friends Meeting (the closest thing the silent-meeting Quakers have to a pastor), and become one of the leaders for the annual, magical Women's DreamQuest.

I'm growing, for sure. But this dream shows me I have a pile, a big stack, boxes and boxes of work yet to do.

DREAM JOURNAL

The poetry practice gave me the first good run at milking the holy cow, but it didn't end there. In the dark time of my marriage, I worked through *The Artist's Way* with my good friend Peg. It's a twelve-week program in creativity by Julia Cameron. A key part of it is doing "morning pages." Three hand-written pages every morning, don't stop, write whatever comes. This was so enlivening, such a clear encounter with the cow, that decades later I am still doing it every day. I do the Katie inquiry-work, I honor the bright spots from the day before, I list ten things I want, I write poems — and I record my dreams.

There are lots of ways to keep track of dreams. Many people keep a separate dream journal, and even illustrate them with collage or paint or drawing. I'd like to do that, but mostly I just write down my dreams as I journal in the morning. This was Jeremy's practice too, and I learned something from him which kicked my dreamwork up a notch. It's a book that I keep specifically as an index. *A Dream Title Index*. When I'm done with a journal, I transcribe the titles of the dreams in that journal into the index. On the facing page I make notes about what was happening in my waking life at the time of each dream. Sometimes I add a few words to enrich my memory of the dream. With this index I can look back and easily locate a dream among the stacks of journals. And I can scan through for themes and recurring stories. This has deepened my ability to track my dream life, and it's hard to imagine how I could have written this book without it.

THE NEW LAW — *Dream*

August 2006
53 years old

A new law is in the works, but the voters haven't passed it. It's been stalled for about ten years. It would enable development along a big road, out near our house. The city agency that has proposed the law zooms in on a scene that explains why the neighbors haven't voted for the law.

It would mean tearing down a messy, junky house with dead mattresses on the porch, but the old apple orchard around the house would also be cut down. They hate to lose that lovely overgrown orchard. Now it's time, however. The law has been stalled long enough. The neighbors are ready to vote for it. It will create some new greenspaces as well as housing, so that helps them feel better about the loss of the orchard.

THE NEW LAW — *Reflection*

I have this dream during a vacation at the beach with my family. It marks a turning point. The ruling forces in me—represented by the city—are done waiting. I've been stalling for ten years. Time for new developments.

But what exactly am I being asked to do? What is the new law? I can't quite accept that it is time to leave. Three years of counseling, with two different counselors, have gotten us more or less nowhere. Jack goes with me, but he doesn't take it seriously.

As I watch the crab boats puttering around Netarts Bay and write in my journal, as the girls play in the yard and Jack chops firewood, one thing becomes clear. I need some money of my own. I have to get a job.

The tone of this dream is calm. They're not upset with me. "We get it," they say. "We know why you haven't been able to leave Jack. It *is* a lot to lose. Your little farm is alive, enchanted and wild, an acre and a half for children to run around in, to play with ducklings and to swing on the long swing in the huge old apple tree. The junky house—your marriage—is trashed, and has to go, but we honor the sweet stuff you were trying to save, and the cost of losing it." No judgement at all from the dream team. But they are firm on the time-for-change message.

We come home from the beach, apples fall off the big tree, the girls go back to the Earth School. While I chop apples for applesauce, I ponder what kind of job I want. Should I cook? Teach? Work for a nonprofit? I'm headed to Hungary and Italy in the middle of October, and can't start work until after that, so I fix my resume and keep up with my chores, starting to feel the feathers of freedom in my hair.

PARI, ITALY

October 2006

If you climb up and up along the narrow red streets of Pari, a hill town in Tuscany, you come to a plaza near the bell tower where you can look out across the golden Italian countryside, studded with cypress trees, until it hazes into light. A few steps down from that plaza is a tiny apartment where I live for ten days in 2006.

My friend Marie, who is teaching English in Hungary, gifted me this trip, plane tickets and all. I fly to Budapest, and we take an overnight train to Florence, where her boyfriend, Carlo, picks us up. I have come to pick olives on Carlo's farm, but also to drink in the long sightlines, to hover over my life from high up and far away. What might be visible from this place that I can't see from inside the full catastrophe at home?

It is ten days of Italian heaven. Olive picking is friendly work, pulling green olives off long branches to fall into tarps on the ground. The olive leaves are soft, like the ears of deer; the food at the farm is unforgettable, the sunlight old and fresh at the same time. I love walking a mile downhill every morning through the forest to the farm, avoiding boar hunters with their rifles and camo; love the tiny curving streets of this red town, the sense of long inhabitation, the deep views, the ringing of the bell.

I love, too, a moment just before we get to Pari. We've been driving for a couple of hours, it is night, and Carlo suddenly pulls over at Terme di Petriolo, an ancient hot springs. It is dark and quiet. Sulfur-smelling hot water bubbles out of the hillside. Marie and Carlo lie down in a stone-lined pool, and I feel my way down the steep path, over slippery rocks, past naked wet people, to the place where hot water hits the river, running wide under a Roman bridge. I swim through the mist and stretch out. The river reaches up to my chin. The pitch-black ice-cold silent river flows along, the river of change.

I work in the olive grove every day until November 1, All Saints Day. That day, I tell Carlo I want the day off. I am going to do some dreamwork in my apartment. Four dreams have come over the last four nights. I feel them bubbling.

FOUR DREAMS IN PARI

October 2006
53 years old

Looking for Work

A woman is looking for work on my behalf.

She asks, "Would you be willing to work as a full-time teacher?"

I say yes.

About to Die

I arrive at a doctor's clinic. There's a sense of impending crisis, though all is quiet in the streets. On a TV screen an announcer reads from a press release, telling us that the crisis is worldwide, originating in the Nile Delta. A nurse herds us down the street and into a school auditorium. People are calm, but it's clear we're all going to die. I talk to a scared man and tell him that death is safe.

The Blue Girl and the Kitten

A Quaker judge and I try to rescue a kitten that has been stuck in an attic for years. We learn about this from a press release in the newspaper. As we climb the ladder we get unexpected help from a blue girl, a three-foot-tall wooden doll who seems dead but is not. She opens her eyes and is vividly alive.

Looking for the Girls' New School

I look for my children, who are going to a new school. Jack makes a big mess with the water heater project, and I'm mad at him.

Surely these dreams hold clues to my questions: Is it time to leave the marriage? What will happen to the girls? Where will we live? Will we be okay?

[I have to note as I write this that I wish the poor girl would just get a move on. Jeez.]

I scribble, study, look for overlaps between the dreams. Fog fills the valley and whitens the windows as I write and write. I work and ponder for a few hours.

I notice a couple of cool puns:

"Press release" appears in two dreams: that is, *press* the *release* button.

The global catastrophe that is upon us has its roots in the Nile: *de nial*.

The dreams as a group remind me of the *New Law* dream, both in compassion and urgency: "Time to move along now, honey." The main quality of these dreams is helpfulness. The woman looking for work on my behalf, the Quaker judge and blue doll rescuing the kitten, the kind people herding us to the school.

I sit at the little desk with the fog swirling outside, getting sleepy. I end by condensing each dream down to a single sentence, in order to feel the specific punch of it. That goes okay, but then I try to mash all *four* dreams into one sentence. No good at all. My best attempt (and it's not remotely a single sentence) is:

Something is pending: about to happen. I get help from unexpected sources, much behind-the-scenes help. I am worried about getting back to the girls on time and mad at my husband. The school where we are assembling and waiting is the girls' new school that I am trying to find.

Worn out by brainwork, I lie down and take a nap. And have a short amazing dream.

GIVE UP — *Dream*

November 1, 2006, nap.
Pari, Italy
53 years old

I enter a room. Hanging over the door is a banner with the single sentence summary that I have been looking for.

Give up — it's all being taken care of.

I tell the story to a guy standing nearby:
"I had the day off to do some dreamwork, and worked on four dreams. I managed to condense each one into a sentence. Then I tried to get a single sentence summary of all four together, but I couldn't do it. I was tired, so I took a nap. As soon as I fell asleep, the answer appeared on that banner."
He shakes his head, impressed.

It's hard to convey the importance of this dream. It seems so simple, just a little wren, but it steps on my chest with the weight of a god. It pulls back the veil of everyday conditions and reveals, for a second, an impossible wild power behind the curtain.

I have a persistent belief that *I need to know what to do.* (You might have this belief as well. I notice my daughters do.) It doesn't seem like a story at all, but plain old reality. I think I have to make decisions, plan, fret, predict.

But this dream says, LISTEN UP!

STOP THAT!

IT'S ALL BEING TAKEN CARE OF!

They don't bother to code their message. They write it in English, on a banner, and make me tell the story to someone so I won't forget it.

When I look in the rearview mirror, I see how right they were: how tenderly, even miraculously, my stuff was taken care of.

For one thing, the job. The woman who was looking for work on my behalf? Who wanted to know if I'd be willing to take a job as a full-time teacher?

When I get back from Italy, my friend René—the tall man I met on the beach on the morning of the *Magical Tools* dream—suggests that I talk to the nuns who run the Earth School. I have zero Montessori training, so it seems like a long shot, but when I approach Mother Francine just before Christmas and tell her I am looking for work, she takes my hand, looks me in the eye and says, "We don't have anything right now—but don't take another job."

In January a Children's House teacher breaks her leg and I substitute for her, spending a sweet month with preschoolers. Just as that ends, the middle school humanities teacher gets arrested. He is forbidden to come on campus, but no one tells the parents why. They start to freak out.

"We can't tell you what it was, but it's nothing to do with children," the nuns insist. Still, they need to calm the parents, bring in someone they trust, and hmm . . . Can Tina teach humanities?

She can. In fact, it is the only professional job in the school she is qualified for. She will even get to teach peace studies, which thrills the Quaker activist in her.

Every bit of my conundrum is tended to, not just the job. The girls and I move in with my dad and stepmother in the old Victorian next to David's house, where I used to live with Sam. It is a true refuge. And I fall in love.

It is great, but so weird. *Who* is taking care of it?

Here's the thing. I play some part in it—mysteriously, but truly—I can't just lie on the couch and expect it all to be taken care of, la la la. I participate as some kind of co-creator, but how does it work? This is an important question and gets sharper as I look back at the winding rivers of my life. I honestly don't know. I suspect it has to do with increasing my need. Being willing to long for what I truly, nakedly long for. Kindling the sparks of desire. Every day writing down ten things I want. Something like that.

As Martin Buber put it in *I and Thou*:

> *. . . Then he intervenes no more, but at the same time, he does not let things merely happen. He listens to what is emerging from himself, to the course of being in the world; not in order to be supported by it, but in order to bring it to reality as it desires.*

THE FAUN'S GARDEN — *Dream*

June 3, 2007
53 years old

I stand at the back of an auditorium in an old school building, watching my students in a dress rehearsal of a play. It's informal, relaxed, pleasant.

A student announces over the loudspeaker: "Tina has been appointed to the ruling council." Then comes another one: "She's been taken off, because she can't yell."

The announcements are serious, but playful too.

Outside on the grass, I sit in a circle of the students' parents. We throw a tube of sunscreen around the circle. Someone tosses it to me. I don't take any, just throw it quickly on, but the cap comes loose, and a lot of it squirts out onto the woman's lap where it lands. I rush over and try to scrape it off her white pants. "I think it will be okay," I say. She is upset, expecting me to clean it up and save it.

"I'd just throw it away," she says, "except I heard someone say it's very expensive."

I feel responsible to save this wad of cold cream that I have wiped up. (More than the tube held, actually.) I head toward the kitchen to get a pint or quart jar. The cream is now on my back, in a big pile.

A third announcement:

"You're back on as president of the council, because yelling is not required."

I walk along the hall with a few students. Two girls and I go up a spiral staircase. We run into some rotten stair boards. I pull one off; it falls to the ground far below. I could jump through the hole but that would scrape the cream off my back, and I'm still trying to save it. I pull up three or four more rotten boards, leaving quite a hole. I look at the ground below and decide I can make it. I jump through.

I'm not hurt. It's a long fall, but the ground is muddy and

I pick myself up. I've forgotten about the cold cream, looking around at this place I've landed. It's a wild garden, with statuary, big stones, overgrown trees.

The faun, whose garden I have jumped into, comes over and says, "It's been a long time since I saw you."

We are old friends, glad to see each other.

I reach out to take his arm; he squeezes my finger. We walk through his beautiful garden. The castle or buildings I just left are black, far-off ruins up against the skyline. I've fallen into a protected, leftover, magical place. A sheltered spot with a familiar dear friend. It reminds me of *The Wind in the Willows*. A different life.

THE FAUN'S GARDEN — *Reflection*

Reading through my journal of the time when I had this dream, my heart aches for Jack, who finally realizes I am serious. He starts to apologize and beg me to stay. Until this moment, evidently, he thought I was just blowing smoke. No wonder almost three years of counseling has failed us. But after years of clawing my way up the side of a well, trying to get his attention, I can't turn around. I am too close to the rim to give up now. I'm getting out. It's over.

The dream comes in early June. I move out August 1. Six months later, I start to date a man who can only be described as a faun—musically gifted, sexually charged, playful, and skittish.

This is one of the strange gifts of recording dreams over the course of years. Sometimes, as with the *Cat-Baby* dream, it's clear that they know things they shouldn't know—things in the future, things at a distance. They knew all about the faun.

I easily recognize the ruined staircase and rotting stairs in this dream as the life my husband and I built that couldn't bear our weight—mine and the two girls with me, our daughters. But I could never get what the cold cream was about.

Now I see it is about sex.

I didn't want to see that cold cream as a sexual image, but of course it is. The tube that squirts white cream onto a woman's lap? As a sexual symbol it's kind of awful. The cream spills out of a tube, not a person. It's *cold*. And expensive. It makes me feel guilty. It cost a lot—(as my marriage did)—and even though it isn't mine, I try to save it. I try to find a jar to put it in: *ajar*—I'm trying to find an opening. I tear the stairs up and make my own opening, in the end. And jump into another place, a garden where the sex will be friendly, surprising, and full of delight. The contrast between these two versions of sex, in one dream, is harsh. From cold, expensive, guilt-ridden, impersonal, to safe, magical, exploratory, loving. Ouch.

Why, in this dream, do the students keep changing their

mind about whether I'm on or off the ruling council? Evidently some part of me was not clear about whether I needed to get mad to leave Jack.

In fact, no. Yelling was not required, after all. Just make a hole, and jump.

HAWKEYE

Whew. The release. What she couldn't do for herself, she did for her daughters.
She feels this sailing joy, and she deserves to!

But oh she is a stubborn little nut.

What do we do for her now?

Let her be happy for a while. Let's all just rest. That was a big push.
She has arrived in this friendly meadow, green and open.
The mountains loom ahead of her, but no rush.

Let her explore the field, have some sweet sex, enjoy teaching, cuddle her daughters. Her younger sisters are going to die in a few years, and we can help her to be awake for that. But here's a chance for her to gather strength and good cheer, waterproof her boots and repack her pack, before we go on up.

INTERMISSION

A good moment for us—you, dear reader, and me—to raise a glass of strong red Tuscan wine. I am released from my promise never to touch alcohol, a promise I kept for fourteen years. We can toast to hard work, the long scramble that got me out of my marriage. The next few years, as Hawkeye says, will give me a chance to rest, before the next big wave of dreams, and change.

L'chaim!

EIGHT
In which I glimpse a god

THE FAUN — LOVE AFFAIR

March 28, 2008
54 years old

Five months after my dream of jumping into the faun's garden, I meet Will at a Halloween party. I feel a jolt of attraction to his gentle, intelligent face. At the break, he comes over. He somehow mentions that he worked on archaeological digs in England in his youth.

"Me, too!" I say. "How crazy is that!" This is a sudden, strong cord between us. We share a passion for deep time, the magic of ancient monuments, the shadowy tracks of prehistory.

A few months after the Halloween party, he breaks up with his girlfriend and reaches out to me. We go for hikes, kiss under the trees on the forest trail. Eventually he takes me to his house.

I am stunned. His rooms have the overgrown, secret, haunted, familiar magic that pervaded the faun's garden in my dream—old furniture, bronze statues on his mantelpiece, musical instruments on the wall. The blue bookshelves full of poetry, the silent etchings of English landscapes, and the wide flagstones of his fireplace hearth are balm after the piles of junk and unfinished projects at my house with Jack.

One evening in his bedroom Will tells me a story about his childhood. He lived in England for a year when he was ten. His father, like mine, was a college professor and went there on a teaching-exchange program.

"There was a children's author living in the village who was friends with my mother. She used to invite me over for tea."

I wave at him to stop. The hair is rising on the back of my neck and a humming noise has started in my head. I can feel what is coming.

He doesn't stop or even notice my agitation. "Her name was Kathleen Hale." He keeps talking, rambling, describing how he would get dressed up to visit this old lady.

I am shaking. I go out to stand in the hall.

"Where are you going?" he asks, confused.

We are living through this moment from two different planets. He is randomly reminiscing; I am undone.

Kathleen Hale was the author of my favorite magical childhood books about Orlando the Marmalade Cat, the ones I did a rare-book search for at Pendle Hill. I've never met anyone who had even heard of her. That he had lived in her village and gone to her cottage for tea is so unexpected that I feel like the gods have snicked us together like magnets.

A few days later, while he is cooking dinner, I kneel and touch my forehead to the floor of his bedroom, raw with gratitude. He is in the kitchen and doesn't see or know. Kneeling there, tears in my eyes, I bless all the beings and turns in the road that allowed me to find my way into the refuge of his arms and his house. It isn't just the loving sex, though that is a revelation. It is that he knows me, gets me, sees me—as the Witta, or a haunting melody—someone with a foot in another world. His enthusiasm for me is the clearest, sweetest water to my sore soul. The smells of garlic and hot oil waft down the hall while I feel the hardwood floor on my forehead and the groundlessness of gratitude in my chest.

I keenly feel the presence of my *Faun's Garden* dream. I have jumped out of my old life into a new one, a hidden, overgrown, marvelous garden, where this playful, sexy being lives. I tell Will the dream, and he likes it so much that he has a friend make me a delicate porcelain statue of a faun.

It would have been easy to remember that a faun is a fluid, chancy, good-times creature—not the kind to settle down and get married. But this doesn't occur to me.

For eight years, I stay at Will's house every other week, when my daughters are with their dad, and it seems to work. Not that we are perfect together. He isn't a risk taker, doesn't have a job, is content to burrow down in his house at the end of the road. I am often frustrated that he doesn't choose a bigger life. Nonetheless, thanks to my sense that something like fate has smacked us together, I feel all in.

We travel to England. We rent a cottage near Stow-on-the-Wold and find our way across grassy fields and down tiny lanes to Neolithic hill forts, Wayland Smithy, the White Horse of Uffington, pubs with Morris dancers in the yard, circles of standing stones, the lacy stone cloisters of Oxford and Gloucester. We both dive into this quest for magic and reverence in the English landscape. It is a tune we both can hear. It led us both, after all, to work on digs in England when we were young.

We also journey together through the deaths of my younger sisters, Kathryn and Barbara, who die in the fall of 2010.

Kathryn has leukemia, though she doesn't die of it; she gets a lung infection she can't fight off because chemo has shattered her immune system. I sit at her bedside the night she is dying, holding her hand. She has a morphine pump and tries not to press it. Her lungs are filling with fluid and she knows it. She wants to walk out of this world awake, but she is scared.

She says, "Help me."

In that moment I am as present as I've ever been. I sing "Row, Row, Row Your Boat" with her and wish I knew more songs. I feel how her soul has saturated the room with love, like the salt-rich lagoons in Baja where the gray whales go to calve. "It's holding you, you're safe, you're like a baby whale who can't sink. There's so much love in here," I tell her.

At four in the morning, I take a nap on the floor, and when I wake up she is gone.

Barbara goes out slowly, a few weeks later, in her sleep. She has a brain tumor, after some years of battling bone and breast cancer. I have such a strong sense that they left together on purpose, that Kathryn went first in order to be there when Barbara arrived.

I am sad, and also furious. Not that they left, but that I had to go on teaching while they were dying. The hell with that, I decide. I'm done working for someone else. If anybody else dies, I want to be there, making smoothies, brushing hair, telling bad jokes, singing, tending—like my sweet brother, Richard. Since he is his own boss, he was able to show up for our sisters as much as he chose. Will holds me as I cry through that winter and spring.

I quit my teaching job at the Earth School and launch into working for myself. Why not? I've accumulated enough tools to fill the back of a spiritual pickup truck. I teach Byron Katie's Work and see clients for spiritual direction and life coaching. I officiate at weddings. I tutor kids from my former school. I help people publish books of poetry and run the odd dream workshop. It is not much money, but enough to live on. And I join the Threshold Choir, a group of women who sing at the bedsides of people who are dying, where I learn a whole raft of lovely songs that I could have sung to my sister.

I make a journey with nine other women from the Threshold Choir to Bali and Thailand in the spring of 2012, a trip woven entirely of blessings. It's so delicious to sing all the time: every morning, every evening, and whenever we say goodbye to anyone. The island of Bali feels beloved, sacred. It's full of little shrines, statues wearing flowers and aprons, monkeys, monks, spicy noodles, bright silk, secret pools.

The most extraordinary hour of the trip takes place in Thailand, in the jungle north of Chiang Mai, at an elephant rescue park. We've been invited here to sing to the elephants, particularly the baby Faa Mai, three years old. As we stand together in the dusty, bamboo-strewn pen singing our gentle songs, Faa Mai puts her trunk in her mouth, slowly closes her long-lashed eyes, and lies down. One of her huge aunties comes and stands over her, straddling her. It is a moment, like touching the barnacled whale in Scammon's Lagoon, of communion, of belonging on this Earth.

It is a quiet period for dreaming, then and for a couple more years. And in 2014 the big dreams start to come.

APOLLO'S WORLD – *Dream*

February 23, 2014
60 years old

I'm in a city, looking out the window in the evening. The sun is rising in a deep blue twilight sky. A figure, with an invisible body but outlined in light, jumps and somersaults away into the darkness. He is Apollo, and maybe Kokopelli as well. A god, tumbling and playing.

I open the door to a world transformed. It's a different city, in an earlier time. People drive very old cars, wear different clothing. It's like a play or movie but entire, more real than a movie set and yet clearly *created*. It's amazing, wonderful. I wonder if there's a faint hint of snow in the air—yes! It starts to snow, and I'm thrilled. I kneel down in the street in gratitude, touch my forehead to the ground.

A thin, dark-haired young man here likes me and my gratitude. He offers me his arm as we go walking in this new world. I marvel at it. He says, "You made it."

That doesn't seem possible, and I say, "No, Apollo made it."

I love walking through it with him—everything is so lovely, the snow, the strange old cars. I am surprised this young man chose me; he seems special, and I am ordinary, but he has.

Back at the house, I am naked and embracing another man. At first I think this is a conflict with loving the young thin man, but it doesn't seem to be.

Later I see some women on TV. They are exquisite, as if the same hand who has made this entire world has glamorized them. One of them likes the same young man. The show ends and she pulls out her phone. I know she's calling him. I've been trying to call him, too, looking for his number. I think: *No way can I compete with that level of beauty.*

Then he shows up at our house! I'm so happy. I say, "I was just trying to call you, looking for your number." He gives it to me. "221-7759. Now you have it."

Outside, snow covers the trees. It's night. I touch the snow and it's not cold. I say, "It's still there, the fake snow." I'm thrilled and amazed that the alternate world is still going on.

Snow that isn't cold? Sun rising in the evening sky? Loving two men at the same time? Wrong. Wrong. Wrong. Yet the enchantment of this alternate place buckled me at the knees.

It's hard for me to believe that I made this world. I did, of course. I dreamed it. But I can't admit it inside the dream. I have to give Apollo the credit. Something similar to the *Witta* dream is in play here: I *want* to feel my creative energy flow and take shape, but I am wary of it, too. When I think of the Witta's fiery surge of power, or of agreeing with the young man who tells me I made this alternate world, I feel myself duck and slide away. I hate to be seen as arrogant. I don't want to be lopped off at the knees as a tall poppy. I'm afraid that if I allow myself to shine, I will get attacked or shamed.

And yet my dreams tell me something else. You're brave, they say. Come on, you walnut, stand up. Admit what you can do. It's almost more arrogant *not* to try.

I hunted through my journals for clues to the origin of this dream. My life was tootling along. I was more or less happy with Will, my girls were doing fine. No big conflicts or crises or problems—so what on earth gave me this potent dream?

A book. I'd just read *Being Wrong*, by Kathryn Schulz.

My oldest, strongest story—the moldiest, crabbiest box in that Enron room in the *Knights Errant* dream—is *"I need to get it right."* I wish I knew the number of times I have questioned that thought. Since I started following Byron Katie's suggestion to have The Work for breakfast, I have questioned a few thousand thoughts (ten years, 365 days a year). But not a few thousand *different* thoughts—I have a fun little repertoire of twenty or so that keep tripping me up. Often, it is some form of "I need to get it right." Over time, the belief has eased up, but it can still bite me.

Whenever I have to negotiate with Jack or call the IRS, I feel that cold sharp fear of getting it wrong. It doesn't show up around my daughters, or Will—there I feel confident, like a normal human being. But in the presence of a capricious, complex power or bureaucracy, my insides become a crouching, hiding child, voicelessly saying, "Don't hurt me!" Not too hard to guess where this came from. When my dad shouted at us, I froze. I began to anticipate, watch, guard myself, offer to help before being asked, stay quiet, listen. What did I know? I thought "getting it right" was possible, and might keep me safe.

Being Wrong gave me a thrilling break from that. Schulz, who calls herself a wrongologist, says that the power to get things wrong is a splendid and amusing feature of being human. Our need to get it right, she says, functions as a tiny terrified box. Her book melted my own tiny box away, for a few weeks after I read it.

That blast of relief, thank you Kathryn Schulz, ignited this whopper of a dream. It tells me what might be possible if I could slide out of that box for good. Not to deny that being wrong can be costly. Itchy. Scary. But it can also open the window to a space where a god is dancing and tumbling, outlined in light. A space big enough to fly in.

BECOMING A DREAMWORKER

I've applied to Jeremy Taylor's program, the Marin Institute of Projective Dreamwork, to be certified as a dreamworker! I'm excited. He has a list of requirements—coursework, mentorship, hosting a dream group, and so on. I send him an account of what I have already done: two Dream Teacher trainings with the shamanic dreamworker Robert Moss and running our dream group for the last ten years. But I figure I have a year or so of work still to go, including some dreamwork sessions with Jeremy over Skype. We make a date to talk on the phone. Two days before our call, I have a dream.

JEREMY'S CIRCUS — *Dream*

September 1, 2014
61 years old

It's time for my interview with Jeremy Taylor to enroll in his dreamwork certification program. Jeremy asks me a few questions along the lines of "Who are you?" But we are interrupted. When I get back, he is gone.

I walk through his building into a high, gorgeous hall of fabric. The walls are made of hundreds of huge rolls of fabric, fluttering and moving. Some rolls are changing color.

I go outside. I sit on a log with someone who I think is Jeremy but turns out to be his wife, Kathryn. She goes over my paperwork, checking off the things I've already completed, and she says, "It doesn't look like you've met the Move Your Body requirement."

I say, "But I dance twice a week!" and then wonder if I'm telling the truth. Do I?

She's hard to see—the light behind her is so bright. I blink and blink, can't keep my eyes open. That's why I thought she was Jeremy at first. Finally, I ask if we can go inside so I can see better. Before we get up, she points out a man doing magic. He's standing on a big log, which slowly morphs into a boat around him. At the same time, it becomes a man's huge naked body. I can see the relaxed penis and the hands inside the bark.

Instead of going in, we go over to a big field with a steep hillside—to "move our bodies." Running up and down this green hill are a dozen or so strange beings, like black upside-down brooms. Their heads are wispy, black, and feathery, and their bodies thin as broomsticks. Servants of some kind. I try running up the hill but don't make it. The day and place are beautiful, shining. Between the hall of fabric, the man-boat magic, these odd black beings, and the size of the whole operation, I'm reminded of Cirque du Soleil—the force and reach of what they are engaged in. An immense imaginative power at work.

We go indoors. Kathryn wants me to catch the long-distance bus, which is just pulling up outside. I think the driver sees me, but I'm not sure he stops to let me on.

Two days after this dream, I call Jeremy and have the conversation in waking life that we began in the dream. I make the call from a quiet hospital courtyard; I've just been to see a doctor about my eye.

That dazzling light in the dream, too bright to look at, spilled out of the dream and I woke with a painful sensitivity to light. I thought it was iritis, a serious inflammation of the iris that I'd had a few times before, but the doctor said it was an incipient sty, and told me to hold a hot hard-boiled egg against it. The whole dream shimmers with wild and magic energy, but that encounter with the light is the moment of most power.

I am nervous and excited as I call Jeremy from the courtyard. I had sent him a copy of the dream, and we talk about it a little—he loves the "Move Your Body" assignment (not an actual requirement for his program)— and then he says, "You're good to go, Tina! You've done all the stuff you need to do. You're certified."

"What?"

"But you still might want to do dreamwork with me over Skype. It's a little cheaper if you aren't yet certified, but are you okay with being certified and doing it anyway?"

"Of course, Jeremy." I am laughing, almost crying.

The adventure I set out on to become a professional dreamworker opens out that day into a wild space, the space described by the dream: a thrilling, magical community with a range of imagination to rival Cirque du Soleil. It is a place of rippling, living material—the raw beautiful fabric of our lives. It is a place of transformation, where a tree is a boat is a living man; of mysterious helpers like tiny agile black palm trees; of a brightness too intense to look at, out of which someone is speaking to me.

This bright being is multilayered. It is Jeremy; it is his wife, Kathryn; it is my dead, glorious sister Kathryn; it is me; it is the characters who write my dreams. This is my "bright shadow."

That is, the shining potential in me that I have not claimed, that is hard for me to look at. But it lives here, in this splendid strange space of dreams and dreamwork. Right here is the stop where I can catch the long-distance bus. This work, the dream tells me, will take me a long way. Maybe all the way to the mountains from which the wind of deep childhood blows.

FARAWAY PLANET — *Dream*

December 1, 2014
61 years old

I'm on a faraway planet with my friend Anita and a small group of people. We've left Earth because of impending disaster there, which may also be impending on this new planet.

I mention to the other people that we are never getting back to Earth, which surprises them.

"Why not?" they ask.

"Earthquakes, storms, big floods, rising seas." I try to paint a picture for them. I thought they understood when we left, but apparently not. Though Anita is the leader, I knew the deal all along. The water is rising on this planet, too. We have limited time, possibly only months to live. But maybe longer than we would have had on Earth.

I look up at the brilliant night sky and ask, "Can we see Earth from here?"

As I speak, I realize, no, of course not, it's in a whole other galaxy. The sky is dense with stars and nebulae.

But Anita says, "Look! There's Venus!" or maybe she says "Evening Star."

I look. A part of the sky is roiling; something incredible is happening—stars and constellations are moving around, shifting/swirling, in one region of the sky. It is mind-blowing.

FARAWAY PLANET — *Reflection*

My lord, what a morning, when the stars begin to fall.
— Traditional song

Jeremy and I work this dream over Skype. His cheerful face, gray hair, and little purple hat are framed by piles and towers of books behind him.

He tells me, "It is very good news that you are dreaming about the planetary crisis, because we never dream about problems we can't do anything about.

"The forces of evolution," he goes on, "are aware of the crisis that incomplete human consciousness has created and are working to teach us. They are evolving the collective — especially our capacity for compassion."

This idea sticks in my gizzard a bit. I respect Jeremy so much, but how can he make a claim like that? It reminds me of Gonzo's comment about the magical tool in my dream: "Oh, I know what that is." This confidence — not quite arrogance, but an odd, breezy (male?) assurance, born of long travel in the invisible world — feels too assured.

Really, Jeremy? How do you *know*?

The "forces of evolution" — What do they look like when they're at home?

And whoever or whatever they are, they're actually concerned about climate change and war, violence and rising seas? They want to wake humanity up in time to avert complete wipeout? And they employ our dreams to do it? Crediting the universe and evolution with intentional intelligence and agency: with the desire, the will, and the ability, to send us evolutionary dreams: Really?

I shake my head, trying to get this to land somewhere.

I love Jeremy. Sitting there in his purple hat and scholar's cave, he seems as wise as a tree. I know he's worked with thousands of people and their dreams over fifty-odd years. If he says he's been watching evolution in action, I want to believe him. What a huge, hopeful, odd idea. I remain skeptical but also feel the threads of a slight thrill. What if it *is* true? What if dreams can actually help us to change—change enough, soon enough, to keep us from burning the place down?

The thing is, this dream does alter me, and becomes evidence for Jeremy's assertion. When it first comes, and I wake with the taste of wonder in my mouth, I don't know how to even start to think about it. I've been *so* far away. But over time I can feel it working on me.

This dream came to stretch my soul, if that is a stretchable thing. (Which of course it is.) To soften reality in a way that will be unforgettable, jaw-dropping, almost shattering—not to scare me, but to widen me with a beauty that breaks the imagination. It came to take me apart. To let me know that even the steadiest, most reliable realms—like the night sky—are in play. Are in motion. Will respond to my gaze. Everything, if you look at it, flows and bubbles and is alive.

I think this touches on what Jeremy means with his "forces of evolution." The next few dreams in this book all share this wild flavor, as do *Apollo's World* and *Jeremy's Circus*. They shiver with an untranslatable shapeshifting energy. They extend an invitation to rethink reality. The awe I experience standing in another galaxy, looking back toward Earth, and seeing the constellations bubble and flow, altered me. I can feel it to this day. It changed my body in the direction of something new. I am being incubated by these dreams, like a chick inside an egg. Kept warm by the steady heat of some great power, that, as Gerard Manley Hopkins put it, "over the bent/World broods with warm breast and with ah! bright wings."

Later I realize that in this dream we must be (in some way) standing on Earth, because from where else would we be able to see Venus? This dream places me in two worlds at once: at home on our planet in crisis and far far far away, far enough to explode my parochial view as an Earthling.

Jeremy, it turns out, is not the only one to suggest that dreams are working to evolve us. Montague Ullman, who founded the Dream Laboratory in New York, says: "Perhaps our dreaming consciousness is primarily concerned with the survival of the species, and only secondarily with the individual. Were there any truth to this speculation it would shed a radically different light on the importance of dreams."

BAKER IN THE WOODS – *Dream*

December 24, 2014
61 years old

I'm in a tent in the forest talking to my Quaker friend Rachel. We leave the tent to shop at the bakery right outside. Rachel's been here before, but it's my first time. The baker is Armenian. He has a glass counter and shelves full of bread out in the middle of a clearing.

I talk to the baker and two other men. He shifts back and forth from being a baker to a shaman/magician: in and out of the clearing, in and out of normal clothing and ceremonial clothing. He does magic which I can't exactly recall. It is strong, strange, intense. One man, lying on the ground naked, is aroused. His body is beautiful and decked with flowers and leaves. He touches himself and I lie on him at some point. Sexual, ritualistic, wonderful.

The baker diagnoses me as needing a certain big flattish uncut loaf. I tear off a piece. It's softer and whiter than I expected, not chewy. I want to buy some baklava. He has some bags on the counter but they are already sold. He blends various bits together to make a new batch. I eat some—it's incredible, amazing, the best I've ever had.

A tree trunk in his clearing stands about ten feet high and ten to fifteen feet around. I look through holes in it, made by squirrels or birds, and see it's hollow inside. As I look, the bark starts to *respond*—to bubble, swell, move—just like the galaxies in the *Faraway Planet* dream—and to reveal pictures, including stars and the Milky Way. This is incredible, jaw-dropping, but apparently needs to stop, as one of the guys (not the baker) comes over and wraps his arms around the trunk, lifts it up, and sets it firmly back on the ground, thump, as if to stop it from flowing. It reverts to normal bark.

BAKER IN THE WOODS — *Reflection*

Over the course of a year a series of magical dreams blaze into my sleeping mind: *Apollo's World, Jeremy's Circus, Faraway Planet,* and then this dream, *Baker in the Woods.* Three more dreams in this series, *Pawprints in the Land, Barge to Quimby Bay,* and *The Cauldron,* are headed my way in the next few months. They are linked, puzzling, empowering, big dreams. Some images recur: stars, logs, magic, transformation, naked men on the ground, solid things that flow in response to my gaze. But the flavor underneath the images interests me even more, though it's a hell of a thing to try to describe. I touch on it in the commentary on *Faraway Planet:* the dreams are changing me, unfolding me. I am being incubated by something behind the scenes, by forces much bigger than me—Jeremy's "forces of evolution," possibly. Something was afoot for sure, and is still afoot as I write, because whatever they were coming to teach me is still in play. It's not over.

But why these dreams at this time? What has activated the giant creative energy of the archetypes? Nothing notable is happening in my waking life—I'm working, trying to help my younger daughter get into college, seeing Will as usual, caring for my parents, reading, writing in my journal, taking a storytelling class. As I look back through my journals, however, for the root of these wild dreams, I begin to see glimmers of courage, of hard questioning. I was turning up some burners that had been on a very low, almost invisible blue flame.

The dreams give me one strong clue in the form of the symbol of the tree trunk, which is sometimes a log. *Log* is another word for *journal.*

I'm a mad and persistent journaler. I write at least three pages every morning. I show up wholeheartedly in those handwritten pages, in my fine small black handwriting. Though at the time of the dreams I'm not high enough off the ground to see the earthquake coming, I keep a good map of the territory as I creep across it, fault lines and all. Occasionally the ground shivers a bit as I write. My log comes to life.

One visible fault line in those journals is a sense of loss about playing small. I read a book around here that kicks me in the ass: *Die Empty,* by Todd Henry. He says: "Use yourself up, so when die you've used your strength, your fullness, every bit of it."

Oh, Tina. If you died now, you wouldn't die empty. Why not? Why are your burners on so low?

My journals of this time are full of questions like this. How do I show up more ardently in every realm of my life, especially work?

Eating the baklava is the most intense moment of this dream. So alive, so rich, the best I've ever had. I look it up and read that phyllo, the paper-thin dough that is layered with butter and nuts to make baklava, is Greek for *leaf,* which of course is also the word for a page. The papery layers of phyllo are the leaves of a book, as well as the leaves of a tree.

When I talk to Jeremy about the baklava, he said that it's very rare to experience *taste* in a dream, and a good sign:

"Actually *eating*—chewing, tasting, swallowing in the dream world—is an even more profound metaphor of psycho-spiritual change than dying," he says. "Have you read anything lately that really nourished you?"

Yeah. *Die Empty.*

The dream reverberates with the transformational, interactive power of reading and writing. Phyllo-leaf-tree-pages-book-log-journal-food. So maybe my way forward, my path toward dying empty, lies through writing? It wouldn't be the first time the dream-writers have suggested that.

I find a couple more things in my journal.

The night before this dream I do a small but important brave thing. I send an email to the members of a board I serve on, asking them to treat one of our members with more compassion and gratitude. This isn't normal for me, taking a stand. I try to sneak away when people start shouting at each other. Once the yelling starts, I sit very still. My face goes blank, my breathing is shallow: "Don't get entangled!" I pretend to be a neutral, grounding presence, but I'm mostly a terrified kid.

At the board meeting, though I can see why some people are mad at the committee member, I can't believe they aren't taking into account all the energy he's given to the group for years. They are missing the mountain of dedication by staring at the mosquito of a late reimbursement request. After the meeting, I can't shake the desire to say that. But I'm scared. I'd be taking sides, a sure way to get entangled, and maybe I'd get yelled, at too. Still. I take a deep breath, send my email, and in the enlarged, risky space of having taken a stand, I go to sleep.

One more fault line:

On December 22, two days before this dream, Will and I talk about whether I should sign the Christmas card for his neighbors.

He says, a little resentfully, "You're *sorta* here, some of the time."

My face flushes, and my stomach clenches. What's that about? I drive to his house every night on the weeks my daughters stay with their dad. I put a lot of effort into seeing him. He never, in our seven years together, has stayed at my house.

"I try hard to be here as much as I can, and not 'sorta' here, either," I say. "It seems like my efforts don't count, don't make a real impact on your loneliness. What do you want?"

He stiffens but then stops and digs a little deeper.

"I'm actually of two minds," he says. "Part of me wants a live-in partner, and the part of me that's wary of being burned again is okay with being a single guy. Free. Don't have expectations, that's what I try to live by."

The tectonic plates of our relationship are catching, grinding, building tension. The strangely shifting sky and bark in this series of dreams invite me to step lightly, to keep my knees soft during the coming quake. Be not afraid, they say: the unstable world can be incredible, magical, wild, beautiful, amazing, alive: everything is in play. Seemingly solid things like the night sky and tree bark can flow under your gaze. Life begets bigger, stranger life.

These dreams are prepping me to have my world upended. I am being invited to dance with change. I have no idea what is coming, but that doesn't matter. It is all in play.

WHAT IS LOVE?

A couple of times in the eight years that Will and I are together, I get to the end of my rope. I'd recall some conversation with him that trailed off into nonsense, and I'd say to myself, *that* is *it*. Enough, already, of listening to him go on about the squirrel in his ceiling or a hole in his hedge or a truck turning around in his driveway — all the little encroachments on his territory. Enough, already, of trying and failing to have the rich, risky conversations that nourish me. Stop whining, Tina. You know you're starving in this stream of shallow talk. It's like trying to live on Cheez-Its. And he's tried, you've both tried, to change this for years now. It's not changing.

So.

Twice, I drive the seven miles to his house with a serious face, adrenaline running hot through my chest and arms. Breakup, here we come.

But both times when I park my car in his driveway and open the heavy red door, he smiles down at me from the kitchen and I melt. The presence of the actual guy overrides all my frustration. It is so odd. Like leaving a movie theater and stepping into the outside air: Oh, *this* is real, this is where the real world is.

He hugs me just as usual, warm and kind; we go into his cluttered kitchen and start dinner. He reports on the squirrel. And there it is again, the dry pressure of frustration around my heart and in my throat. But still! I'm somehow happy to be there, chopping onions, petting his shoulder as I go past, handing him the olive oil. It feels right. I am at home.

Part of me, both times, is just relieved to have avoided a painful conversation. That's not to my credit. I was afraid to tell the truth. But at the time I think, Whew! Near miss! I belong here, on some level that's more important than how we talk (or don't).

In his canopy bed, which we call the *temenos* (a sanctuary dedicated to the gods) we can sometimes talk like regular people. We lie on our backs under the white drape of cloth, held up by zigzags of wide blue ribbon, and chat. We are relaxed. Safe. At one point I suggest, "Maybe we should *only* talk when we're lying down." The bed is terrific. Because, just as it frees him to talk about real things, it frees me into sexual happiness. After lovemaking, I lie with my belly and heart against his back, my arms around his wide, furry chest, my head tucked against him, and feel at home as the moon in the night sky or a duckling under the down of her mother. Comforted to the soul inside my cells.

As the *Moon Man* dream showed, I started on my sexual career fearful, unable to stand in my tower—stay present—for sex. Except for a rare minute or two, I couldn't stand to feel all those feelings arising in my body and my heart. I had a lot of sex but I didn't mix it with love, as if that combination would chemically combust me. It was too much, too vulnerable. I could be in love, or I could be sexual—not at the same time. This went on for years.

But with Will, finally, miraculously, I stop keeping myself apart. I let myself be in love, stay in love, and enjoy sex with him—and let the playful, eyes-open sex be a way in to loving him. That hour after lovemaking where I lean against his back, soft as a fawn in long summer grass, is a kind of heavenly melting that I have not allowed myself to feel before in a long relationship.

This, along with my original hit that the gods had assigned us to each other, sheds light on my inability to leave even when I want to.

Around this time I read a book called *A General Theory of Love*. The three doctors who wrote it assert that our limbic system—the part of our brain that we share with other mammals—governs our loving. Like every mammal, we need to be touched, held, physically bonded, and cared for by another warm furry being. We are born unfinished: our limbic system does not develop without the ongoing, tender connection with our mother. And this is true our whole life. We need each other actually, biologically, physically. We are open-ended: "open loops," they call it. Electricity, so to speak, does not flow—the light bulb in us does not go on—without a deep and holding connection with another person who can complete the loop. As the blurb on the back of the book says: "our nervous systems are not self-contained: from earliest childhood, our brains actually link with those of the people close to us, in a silent rhythm that alters the very structure of our brains, establishes life-long emotional patterns, and makes us, in large part, who we are."

PAWPRINTS IN THE LAND – *Dream*

January 20, 2015
61 years old

I'm looking across a river, talking to my sister-in-law Jacquie about doing archaeology on the green, open farmland over there. Two levels of features are visible from our side of the river. First, we just see the normal human-scale features (old roads, walls). But after we've noticed those, and we shift our focus, we can see through them to giant pawprints in the earth, covered with grass and trees. Each one is the size of a hill, maybe forty or fifty feet across. Even covered with grass, they are clearly the prints of an immense cat. Incredible, unbelievable.

PAWPRINTS IN THE LAND — *Reflection*

This dream rams home what I learned from the book *A General Theory of Love*. It is an awestruck glance into the mystery of the levels of being human. In the dream, as I look across a river at the world, I see *through* the human features of the landscape—the neocortex, as it were—and into the limbic level of our existence, where an unimaginably giant pawprint has created an impression in the earth more far-reaching than the human ones. The great cat who made that print is hundreds of feet high. That hungry, vast being stalks through our muscles and bones. We need each other more than we admit: we are open, unfinished, touch-hungry. We are, on a sometimes hard-to-notice level, animals, stamped with the pawprints of god.

BARGE TO QUIMBY BAY — *Dream*

March 14, 2015
61 years old

I step off a riverbank onto a houseboat gliding by downstream.
It is a barge: low in the water, flat on top, heavy and smooth-
riding. All the house parts are down inside. It glides right along.
Lovely sunny day. I sit on the front with my feet dangling over,
watching the eddies and banks as we float along.

A friendly eight- or ten-year-old boy comes up from below.
I ask him where they're going to dock for the night, as I'll have
to find my own way back.

"Pleve," he says.

"Where is that?"

"Near Quimby."

I don't know where that is either.

We go downstairs and I meet his parents. Dad has long
dreadlocks studded with rubies and red clothes. Very alterna-
tive, warm, and alert.

"I'm Tina." I shake his hand.

"Tina Tau?"

He and his wife look at my ring and conclude it's a garnet.
A nice piece.

"Do you make jewelry?" I ask.

Yes, they say. I ask where they are going and they give the
same answer—Pleve/Quimby. I find some maps and inspect
them. Quimby is a bay and Pleve is a tiny bay inside that bay.
That seems fine, not too far. I just don't want to go on down
past London.

I go back up and can't tell where we are in relation to
Quimby. Have we passed it? I look for landmarks. Up ahead
I see several big bridges; I think that's London. So we haven't
passed London yet; we're okay.

I wake in the joy of it. I have, palpably, just been on that barge, gliding along in the sunlight, strong and low in the water. At ease, happy, and curious.

This is the next to last in the series of seven semi-magical dreams that started with *Apollo's World*. These dreams share a sense of depth and wisdom, expansion, change — of *movement*. The bark moves, stars fall, things widen, shift, change shape: magic is afoot.

A couple of things stand out in this one: *I* am the one being moved. Not the bark, the tree, the night sky — but myself, in the stream of the smooth-flowing river. And then there are the jewels. This dream is full of gems. The red ones are visible — my ring, the rubies in the father's hair — but the diamonds are hidden in the words Pleve and Quimby.

Plevé is a jewelry company specializing in diamonds, and Quimby is a character from the *Simpsons*: "Diamond Joe" Quimby, the mayor of Springfield.

Three years later, talking to a friend about the dream, I draw a picture of the river, of Pleve as a small bay off on the side of Quimby Bay.

I say, "It looks like a breast and a nipple."

"Yes," she says, "and it looks like a ring."

I set my own ring (the garnet one the jewelers admired in the dream) over my drawing. It is exactly the same size. Good grief. Of course it's a ring. A diamond ring! It's an image of shelter within shelter, a cove within a bay: like a marriage, tucked inside the shelter of an extended family. What an encouraging, lovely, sweet dream — of being carried along toward a promise of marriage and intimate shelter. But . . .

That is the opposite of what is about to happen. I am about to fracture. Though I don't know it, my unconscious mind absolutely does, as we will see. So why does this sweet dream, featuring the prospect of finding shelter in a diamond ring, come along just now? And considering that I got the diamond connection with Pleve and Quimby right away, why do I only see the diamond ring in the picture three years later?

This dream, like *Cat-Baby* and some others, falls outside the normal experience of time and place. Sometimes the dreams are reading unconscious currents of my psyche—things my conscious mind won't or can't look at. But sometimes they know things I don't see how they could possibly know.

If my awareness exists in a sphere like an orange, here is the outer level, the orange skin of what I know: Will feels upset by my week-at-a-time absences, and I feel guilty. I want to be whole and have a single, nourishing home, to be part of a committed couple. I don't want to go back and forth between two homes. And in just a few months I can make that happen!

In the white pith under the thin orange skin is another level of knowledge: Poor girl, you're in for a shock. *He doesn't want you to move in!* He doesn't want you to make his home your home. He's going to thwart your plan.

But in the juicy segments at the center of the orange, an even deeper part of me knows—as evidenced by this dream—that I will in time be carried downstream to shelter, to love, to commitment. On the other side of darkness will be "daylight full of small dancing particles," as Rumi puts it. I will find smooth, moving water and a life studded with jewels.

It is as if my dream team is telling me: Before we hand you the really gnarly dreams that will guide you through the breakup, we will show you that *we know you're going to be okay.* You won't realize what this dream is about, right now, but we will make it so lovely that you won't forget it. When you do find yourself floating downstream into love and shelter, you will look back at this dream and realize that some part of you knew all along. That will *amaze* you and help you take your hands off the steering wheel. Because that goddamned steering wheel is not attached to anything. As someone once informed you, it's all being taken care of.

Again I hear them trying to teach me to trust: to ride, to rest, to join the flow.

SLED DOG

I stand in front of a thirties-style vintage microphone looking out at two hundred people, their faces dimmed by the bright stage light in my eyes. I can make out a few people I know, smiling. I begin to tell a story, a true story about my life. I call it "Apprentice to the Mystery."

Partway through the tale, after I tell about the clang-shut ending to my dream of starting a Quaker school, I lean into the mike and sing "Live Up to the Light," the song that pierced my despair during Yearly Meeting thirty years before.

"Live up to the light thou hast," I sing, "and more will be granted thee."

I heard that song on the night that my mission of starting a school ground to a halt. The next morning, I had to turn around and find a new meaning, a new pathway in the world.

And now I stand bright-lit in front of all these people, looking back at the maze-like path I ended up on, with its many turns and defeats and sharp corners.

I wonder aloud to the audience:

Did I, in fact, live up to my light?

Have I done what I wanted to do?

Is it possible I have frittered away my precious life?

That is a hard question to ask, especially out loud and in public.

And yet I give a somewhat honest answer.

"I feel like a sled dog that's been pulling a skateboard around the backyard, when what I want is to be part of the team delivering the serum to Nome."

In case you don't know that story: in 1925 a sled dog relay traveled 674 miles in five and a half days to deliver diphtheria serum to the small town of Nome, Alaska. Twenty mushers and about 120 dogs made the run, known on the radio and in newspaper headlines as The Great Race of Mercy. The modern Iditarod is an homage to that race.

I give myself credit for a dose of honesty, admitting how far I am from being on one of those dogsled teams. But I don't want to end my story on a downbeat. I tell the audience about the little gray mouse that came out and danced for me in the dawn, after my night of despair. And how that dream had led me to become a dreamworker:

"Instead of opening a school, I became a student of the wise being inside me who could come up with such a funny, healing, reconciling dream." I look out at the listening faces. "Living up to the light has meant apprenticing myself to that big space, that mystery, that space of freedom that is both inside and outside me."

Okay. That's true; I did that. But what's true as well is that something is wrong. Over the next few weeks the image of that poor dog with her skateboard burns in my body. I begin to feel a sharp sorrow. I have taken a hard look at my condition and I don't like it.

I've done some good things in my life: been an open-hearted mother to my two orphan girls, eased my sister Kathryn through her death, taught a lot of middle schoolers how to write an essay. But there is a lid on my energy, and a fence around the yard in which I allow myself to run. Some key dimensions are missing from my life, all part of the Great Race of Mercy: a big chewy purposeful project, teammates to share it with, and a need for every ounce of energy I can summon. I long especially for the sense of mission those mushers and dogs had. I *want* that—to be fired up, to turn on all my burners. To die empty.

But I don't know what to do with my longing now that I have named it. I go on as before, for a little while anyway. Still, naming it gets something started. My bigger self—the mystery I've apprenticed myself to—takes me in hand, tells me to lie down, and begins the alchemical process which will take the lid off my energy and give me a real sled to pull. They send me an extraordinary dream.

I'M THE CAULDRON – *Dream*

April 20, 2015
61 years old

I'm in a small drugstore with my younger daughter and the woman who owns the store. The three of us are developing a show: spoken word, singing, and an aerial balancing act with ropes. I'm the one doing the aerial act, the finale. We casually invite a few people. I change into my costume; I have a leotard but no bra, and don't want my breasts to flop around, so I look through the store for an ace-style bandage to wrap around me. I don't find one. I also don't have tights, just bare legs, and at first that bothers me, but I finally decide that's okay—bare feet are better for the act.

People arrive, excited, and sit at first facing the back of the store, where the ropes are set up but then turn their chairs to face the aisle. It gets dark, the store gets larger, and more people come. The show begins.

By the time it's my turn, the people have turned yet again, to face the doorway, the front of the store.

The woman announces: "Now it's time for the Terrible Goat!" She means the main act, the finale.

I joke: "Maybe it's the Laughing Goat!" I wonder how to do it at the front, without the ropes.

Instead of aerial dancing or balancing, I lie down in the doorway in front of the crowd. A woman starts an alchemical ritual. She puts something in my belly that turns it a deep purplish red color. She stirs it with her hand. I can see it. All my torso is a vat of this red, viscous liquid. It is incredible and intense to look down and see myself liquidized and stirred. She asks for a frog and a cauldron, and I say to myself, "I'm the cauldron."

People are rapt. Then she puts some odd quarter-sphere pills, white with a dark center, into a plastic cup of water. It turns black. I'm supposed to go away and drink this over the next hour, then come back, and we will see what's happened to me. The key piece of the ritual is finding out how this liquid will interact with whatever she did before.

I go off walking into a park with David Oates and Merilee. It's daylight. We walk around the elegant overgrown lawns and stop at a stone fountain. I realize I don't have the glass and haven't drunk the potion. We split up and retrace our steps to look for it. I don't find it.

David comes and puts a teeny bit of something on the tip of my tongue.

"Did you find it?" I ask. I don't know whether this is the last bit left in the glass, or some other substance. It's so small, just a grain, but potent.

I'M THE CAULDRON – *Reflection*

> *This Buddha Nature or potential is a seed, a kernel, a germ, a small particle that contains within itself a collection of raw elements. This seed in us is our Consciousness.*
> —Gnostic teaching, radio program,
> *Awakening of the Seed*

This dream shows the power of telling my story in front of all those people, almost naked. In the dream I have bare legs, bare feet, and no bra. In waking life I bare myself at that microphone. I speak a raw truth—to myself even more than to the audience. As it turns out, in both waking and dreaming versions of this experience, it's not a performance so much as a moment of allowing myself to open up. I become an alchemical space, a cauldron.

It is *so* weird, unforgettably weird, to see the woman stirring me, moving that hot, heavy red liquid with her hand. I still feel the strangeness, years later—looking down to see my belly as an open molten vat. The ritual is incomplete: in the dream I'm supposed to go away, drink the black liquid, and come back so everyone can observe the full transformation. But I lose track of the potion, and instead a potent dark grain is placed on my tongue—which may have the condensed power of the whole drink.

What is the black potion? Since David Oates is my writing teacher and Merilee runs my writing group, the potion is connected to writing. Perhaps it is *ink*? Maybe the dream is telling me that to complete my transformation I must write about it.

But evidently, at the time I dream this, my grip on writing is tenuous: I lose the cup. The grain that David places on my tongue, however, is magical. It may have condensed the entire potion into a single seed.

I look up grains placed on the tongue and find all kinds of riches.

Placing the Host on a communicant's tongue.

The mountain-moving faith of a single mustard seed.

Best of all, the "Prioress's Tale" in Chaucer's *Canterbury Tales*. The Prioress tells of a "greyne" that is set on the tongue of a murdered boy, which keeps him alive and allows him to keep singing a holy song to the Virgin Mary. When it is removed, he gets to die and go to Heaven. Scholars argue about what that mysterious "greyne" is. A pearl? A seed? A gemstone? A grain of wheat?

Magical grains with the power to grant life and speech; witches' cauldrons with echoes of a volcanic caldera—we're firmly in the realm of myth here. In Jung's writings, the alchemical cauldron is a symbol of soul transformation. And this dream is in that territory. The fact that I myself am the cauldron, with my belly open, that I get to watch the lava, or blood, or potion being stirred, alerts me that this change is not an intellectual endeavor. It begins in my belly and looks a lot like death.

Like it or not, aware of it or not, I am headed for a big shift. The other six dreams in this series, from *Apollo's World* through *Barge to Quimby Bay*, have ripened me. I can look back through those big dreams and sense it happening. Some key books—*Being Wrong, Die Empty,* and *A General Theory of Love*—have shaken me. I've realized that I am the sled dog pacing in a small yard, that I have way more to give than I am giving. I've admitted this out loud to a big audience. But in order to continue to awaken and change, I need to drink the black potion. That black liquid is not only ink but the darkness in my story, the pain I'm reluctant to admit to. In my desire to have a happy ending, to make everything tidy and sweet, I have become, over the years, a mistress of denial. In the dream I set down the black potion of death. I don't want to drink it. Nonetheless my teacher returns to give me the essence of it, the seed that is both death—the darkness—and the power to speak and sing, even when I am, or should be, dead.

HAWKEYE

She's onto us. Yay, as she puts it.

Well, she's onto a little slice of us.

You're right. She just catches us out of the corner of her eye. But she sees how we are untethered to time and place. And she realizes that we are preparing her for something.

She only realizes that afterwards, as she writes the book.

Give her credit, though. Not everyone could pull that out of the sock even in hindsight.

It is satisfying, isn't it—helping her now? She's not frozen in place, but starting to be fluid.

She's receptive to a visit from Apollo. She can see the pawprints of God, watch the galaxies swell and flower across the night sky. She can be the bloody cauldron and the mysterious grain of consciousness. She tastes the sweetness of the book she's going to write. With more space in her soul, we can play a livelier game with her. Invite her to join the circus, as it were.

She's in for quite a ride.
Yup.

NINE

In which a witch sets herself on fire

TAKE A NUMBER

One hot night in the summer of 2015, I come into a loud, sweaty dance hall looking for Will. It's the final evening of a swing dance workshop. He's been to the whole weekend, and I haven't. When I find him, he looks turned on, alive, handsome. I'm happy to see him. I squeeze his hand. He nods across the room at a woman with a kind face and short gray hair. She smiles at us.

"Kim's sweet on me," he says.

"I'm sweet on you, too," I say.

"Take a number," he says.

"What number?"

"Thirteen."

Oh dear! But I know: I'll fix that. In just a couple of months, when both of my girls are finally in college, I can stay with him full time. I'll give him all the attention he needs.

⁎⁎

Not longer after this night, I have a big dream.

THE PYRE — *Dream*

July 9, 2015
61 years old

I'm in a field in rural England, watching action at a distance. I marvel at how tiny the people look from here. A drama is unfolding: a witch is feeling thwarted by the other villagers. She is so mad that she is going to burn herself up on a sacrificial pyre. She has a birchbark torch. The handle is wood and the flames are made of birchbark.

She's building the pyre. The base is a cube of compressed, living animals, maybe ten or fifteen feet across. On top of that she's built a little house out of driftwood, and she's going to stand on that. When the villagers realize what she's doing they start to run toward her to stop her, and I run too.

I get there and open my arms to extract some of the animals from the cube.

"Just the young animals," I say.

First a little pig jumps into my arms and then a foal, a calf, maybe more. I take my armful of leggy young animals to a nearby pond, where some ducks are swimming, and put them in the water. I hope that taking these animals out will destabilize her structure and make it fall over, but I look back over my shoulder and see a roaring tower of flame.

The fire finally goes out, and then a *huge* black bird, sixty or ninety feet across, with a skeletal white head, flies down over the scene. It is an immense bird of sorrow and death. The whole scene feels like a battlefield or something out of *King Lear*—devastation, all shade and sorrow. The bird hovers over the scene and everything is gray and lost.

Will is there, and I'm trying to get his attention, to show him the bird.

After quite a while, I notice that there are wires on the bird's wings. What?? I look up into the sky, where the wires go. Oh my. It is a huge puppet. I can't see anything up there.

"Who is big enough to run that puppet?" I wonder aloud. "God?"

As I wonder this, I notice that the giant wings are made of black cloth (though I'm pretty sure that at first they were flesh, like bats' wings). As I watch, they move, turn white, and become the canvas sails of a tall ship. The wires become the sails' rigging. The whole bird turns into the ship. It is a big ship in full sail, but sitting on the ground.

Now the scene is all joy. The sun is shining, flags are flying, a band plays, and the queen is on deck. It reminds me of *H.M.S. Pinafore*. The back of the ship is not visible—as if it is still in the wings, like a stage ship. I stand on the ground looking up at the queen, with my little animals behind me in their pond.

And I am invisibly informed that this whole series of events—including the pyre and the black bird—was to bring about this ending. It all happened because someone wanted to see the queen.

I wake in the middle of the night, shaken by this dream, and tell it to Will. Rain patters on his metal roof. In the dark, I can feel him listening hard.

He says, "Weird. I had a dream just now, too. I was also in a valley in rural England. I was on some kind of tour — a fictional tour that you could also go on. I was with some other people and we were building a cob house to protect ourselves from a jet boat explosion on a lake."

Hm, I think. Weird is right. A valley in rural England — a lake — and a jet boat explosion, not unlike a pyre. Strong overlaps with my dream. But what is a fictional tour that you can also go on?

I write both dreams down next morning at his kitchen table. I tell mine to my friend Kirsten as we walk through Laurelhurst Park under the high old fir trees, dappled by sun. We stop to watch the ducks in the lake.

"I don't know," she says. "I wonder if it could be a dream for the culture? Maybe about climate change?"

I agree. It seems so big. I can't see where it fits anywhere into my life.

"It's like Noah's Ark," I say. "Saving all those little animals. And I think of Burning Man. The ritual of burning the Man, to renew the world."

I've just read a story in the *New York Times* about a fire ritual in Northern Ireland. David Best, an American sculptor who builds giant temples to be burned at Burning Man, was invited to build a seventy-two-foot hand-carved wooden tower, overlooking the city of Londonderry, still riven along Catholic and Protestant lines. People walked through the tower, prayed, left messages inside. More than 5,000 people a day, Catholic and Protestant, came through. And on March 21, 2015, the tower burned, while thousands of people stood on the hillside to witness the holy flames.

The story of this ritual caught me by the heart. How

wonderful, how forceful, to use art in this way—to use it mythically, for a sacred purpose. To open a space for grief and wonder and then stand to watch it burn. David Best said his goal was to make the structure "so beautiful that you give up the thing that has been troubling you your whole life."

For the next few months I simmer this *Pyre* dream. What little animals am I trying to save? Am I meant to undertake a project like David Best's healing bonfire? It's all so intense—the terrible roar of the pyre, with the angry woman and the living horses, cows, sheep, all going up in flames—the dark weight of that bird of desolation, and its white skeleton head—the strange inside-out transformation to life and light at the end. But I can't figure out what it wants me to do.

Still hungry for a big, true, full-throated love, I lean toward Will with a little more intensity.

In late September, after Jenny is off to college, I start to stay with him every night. This will cure what he's been complaining about, right?—that he doesn't have enough of my time?

But it doesn't feel like I thought it would. He still treats me like a guest: "Oh, you don't need to empty the dishwasher."

After eight years? I'm not supposed to do chores?

In November I bring it up. We're sitting at the dinner table, eating pot roast and cauliflower. "I'm starting to be confused about where my home is," I say. "Is it where I sleep every night—here with you? Or where my stuff is, over with my folks? I kind of expected that when the girls were gone, this would be my home."

He says, thoughtfully, "I know where your home is—it's over there with your dad and Mary. I'm sorry, but I like my autonomy. But I don't mind you staying here every night."

Well, shit. Doesn't *mind*? I want a partner to be crazy about me. I thought he was. What was all that whining about, then? *Doesn't mind?*

I feel sick, thwarted, angry. I write in my journal. Work my dreams, talk to him. Mutter to myself in the car. I love him and I know he loves me. So what the hell?

I've run into some wall in him that he will not let me pass. But I'm far from giving up on us. The click, the shiver when he talked about Kathleen Hale, and the deep grateful gong that went off in me when we first got together are still alive in my body. I still feel like I belong with him.

In February, I have a clear sharp dream.

THE RUSTY CAR – *Dream*

February 7, 2015
62 years old

I pull into a parking place just outside a house where I live. When I get out of the car I look down and realize it's a wreck. It has no tires—in fact, not even wheels, just square axle ends where wheels should attach. Also: no windshield, no headlights, and no gas tank. It's so rusty that I can push my finger through the skin of the door. I wonder if I can get it to a gas station and if it is in any way repairable. It's a charming shape, an old Morris Minor, the kind of car that enthusiasts might buy and restore. It's small, a one-person car. I wonder what it would cost to even get it going. I've already put $2500 into it and I imagine it would cost at least $2500 more to just get wheels and tires and a windshield on it. But how would I ever get it to a gas station?

I go into the house and find my friend Virginia trying on a dress.

"Come here," I say, "I want you to look at something."

We go into the kitchen, and a couple of other roommates are there, and I ask them to look out the window at the car. I want their opinion: Is this salvageable? Is it worth it?

This dream shows my relationship with Will as a funky rusted-out car without tires or wheels or headlights. Or even an engine! The very metal is compromised — so worn that I can poke my finger through it. It is a cute shape, but rotting away.

So how on earth have I been driving it?

As long as I don't get out and look at the thing, I can drive right along. As I told my dream group when we talked about this dream, "I've been driving a fantasy." However, once I see what it truly is, I can't un-see it: *This car is shot.* Incredibly enough, I keep hoping I'm wrong. I ask my friends in the dream: "Do you think this can be saved?" It all shows how dense — and determined — I am.

This dream gives me a heavy stone in the stomach.

Okay, I get it. This relationship will never take me where I want to go. I've been making it go through sheer pretending.

Shit.

Thirteen days later, wired with adrenaline and anxiety, but following what I believe to be the truth according to the dreamworld, I invite Will to talk.

"Come lie down," I say. Under the white canopy of the *temenos*, my heart beating like a flock of hothouse birds, I tell him, "It seems to me this relationship has reached its natural conclusion."

He holds me. We cry.

"But we'll be friends, right?" he asks.

"Yes, of course."

I pack up and take my clothes home the next day. But I leave my art studio there, filling one room of his house. I don't have anywhere else to put it.

We are going to be friends, after all.

I drive off in the thin February light, feeling a thousand things. Wild chaos in my chest, mostly. Sad and scared and relieved and proud of myself.

KING LEAR

Eleven days after the breakup, I go to a performance of *King Lear* with Will. Someone gave me tickets and I invited him. I could have thought that through a little better. But we are trying to be friends—you know?—and *Lear* seems to fit the moment. Blasted heath, naked in the storm, that seems about right.

We sit in the black box room, waiting for the play to start, and he says, "Women in the dance community are all over me. I feel like fresh meat."

My heart, already raw, crumples like a piece of foil. Shit. Am I the person to hear this complaint? Is that what we are doing?

I can hardly stay in my body after that. Regan and Goneril plot away, the old King watches his power run through his hands like sand, and I sit next to Will with my skin prickling and my face hot. I don't know the hurt I am headed for over the next months. I don't realize that he has already started to date, but the burn in my chest tells me something. My body knows.

A month and a half after the breakup, seven months after the *Pyre* dream, I am eating a plate of blueberry pancakes in a café, writing in my journal. Three giggling little boys play in a booth across from me. Lamps like Moroccan-styled pointed pumpkins glow overhead. The little boys make me think of my life with Jack and how the purpose of that relationship was to take care of our children. That's not what I need in a relationship anymore—but what *do* I want?

"Touch, play, soul-work, adventure, home-building, service, magic. Celebration, hospitality, dreaming and spirit," I write.

I feel a stab of loss. The giant skeleton-headed bird hovering over the gray field sails into my mind, a picture of grief. Something clicks:

"Could that dream of the queen and black bird and pyre be about the breakup?"

The dream shivers into focus in a new way. I eat my pancakes and scribble, now wide awake.

"She—I—had to burn myself up—and all those animals too—(was that my sweet mammalian life with Will?) and go through the BLACK BIRD desolation before it could turn from the black bird's wings to the ship's sails—??"

It seems so obvious now. Of course. But—? I had that dream six months *before* we broke up.

As the sun glimmers through leaves and glass onto my table in the café, I wonder: How did the guys who wrote this dream know so much about what was going to happen, when I myself had no idea?

Telling this story, I keep finding myself in "time's maze," in Wendell Berry's phrase—the mystery of past and present and future, winding and layering together in ways that are hard to see from the ground. I want to do justice to the unfolding of my own saga in everyday time and also allow space for the wisdom, so apparent in my dreams, that sees ahead. To study this dream is to realize, once again, that "I" am not much in control of what is happening. The breakup was not only already known well in advance to some part of me (and to some part of Will as well, as his dream of the fictional tour shows) but the inner purpose of the catastrophe was also known.

After that February conversation in the *temenos* when I said we'd reached our natural conclusion, I felt horrible. Will and I emailed every day and saw each other often. We walked in the Arboretum in slashing rain, and he told me how remarkable I am, how he'd never find anyone like me again. I went home after that walk and cried and cried. The lioness in me, the soft animal that attached itself to him, skin to skin, felt so unhinged. I cried every morning as I wrote.

About a month after the breakup, I drove over to his house with a sleeve of flowers, my bouquet of pain. We lay down to talk.

"I fucked up," I said. "I want to get back together." Looking up at the white canopy. Tears running down my cheeks. Holding hands.

He said, "I'm sorry. Maybe later. But I'm in another relationship now, and I wouldn't hurt her for the world."

There I was on the dismal plain, the valley of the shadow of death.

This all clicks into focus in the café as I write under the pumpkin lamps.

Yes, I think: The witch is me. I have a big, intense energy that the villagers—Will—are afraid of. I am thwarted. But that intense energy has to go somewhere. The pain of being rejected is hot. I burned us down.

Actually, I burned me. Not him. In the dream, only the witch is immolated.

I recall Will's dream from the same night in July.

He gets together with some other people, remember, to build a cob house for protection against the jet-boat explosion. In waking life as well as dream, he finds shelter behind thick walls. He jumps right into a new relationship and refuses to "wallow," as he put it. I let the pain in, while he keeps it at bay.

That birchbark torch that the witch uses to light the pyre? My journal. The cream pages of my journal, covered with lines of tiny black writing, look a lot like birchbark. I use the truth I find in those pages to burn down our sweet, living animal connection, the whole physical ground of our relationship. And the bird of death flies down, and I am left standing in the blackened field. *He's with someone else? He wouldn't hurt her for the world?*

But wait—my pancakes are cold, but the blueberries and maple syrup still taste amazing—the dream ends with flags and music, right? What about that?

The fact that this was all written up and played out in my head seven months ahead of time makes my eyes cross a little. What are those guys up to? They made damn sure I would remember this dream by drenching it in fire, death, intensity. But why so far in advance?

Could it be to help me out in this moment? If they knew back in July all about the pyre and the black bird of pain, maybe I can trust that they have a line on the happy ending? Maybe they knew I'd need some help right now, some encouragement to stay the course. Which I do for sure. But who are they, anyway? *Who's big enough to run that puppet?*

The narrator of the dream says it all happened because someone wanted to see the queen. *I saw her.* That was me, the one who wanted to see her—and the queen, too, is me, just like the witch is. The plot of the dream turns the witch into the queen, by way of fire and desolation.

I stare out the window.

"Well," I write, "that certainly bodes well for how this turns out."

My heart still aches, but I feel I've been handed a great gift as I pay for the pancakes and walk out into parking lot in the windy March morning.

So she's gone over the falls. She's increased her need. We have our work cut out for us.

Actually, *we* cut the work out for *her*, you might better say. That as well.

She is listening so much better than she used to. Still, she tries to force herself to be good. She believes that effort will lead her home—even after we told her to stop.

It took some pretty sharp messages to get her to let go of her fantasy. That dream of the rusty car was a stroke of light.

Yes!

And she is leaning into the big question: *Who's big enough to run that puppet?*

If she can keep her heart on that question, we'll be cooking with gas.

TEN

In which I travel around in time

THE PORTAL — *Waking Dream*

May 2, 2016
62 years old

A waking experience that unfolds like a dream.

I am still in the hard, dark time of my grief about Will. A wounded, expanded intensity in my chest. No longer crying, but fallen into a different kind of grief. Wordless. Not the kind of desperate that turns into tears. Elemental. Stricken. Waves crashing against a cliff.

The last words I write in my journal before going to sleep on May 1:

Caterpillar—chrysalis/mush—butterfly.
I'm in the chrysalis/mush stage. Black Bird.
The ship comes out of the wings.
Find that *Little, Big* quote about the ship.

***

At dawn I bound out of bed to find the passage.

Little, Big, a novel by John Crowley, was my sister Kathryn's favorite book. Since her death, I've read and reread it, with a feeling of holding her hand. It's a giant, surprising story about a family who intermarry with the fairies. The passage I want comes near the end of the book when Auberon, the hero, comes into the kitchen and sees someone sitting there who he thought was long dead.

> *. . . It was as though he had lowered the front of the mirrored wardrobe and found not a bed clothed in patched sheets and an old quilt but a portal, a ship in full sail raising anchor, a windy dawn and an avenue beneath tall trees disappearing out of sight.*
>
> *He shut it up, fearful. He'd had his adventure. He'd*

followed outlandish paths, and hadn't for no good reason given them up. He got up, and clomped to the window in his rubber boots. Unmilked, the goats bewailed in their apartments.

THE PORTAL — *Reflection*

I sit in my low red armchair, letting the passage wash through me, feeling both the shining invitation—the windy dawn, the ship raising sail just off shore, the avenue of trees—and the thud of Auberon's refusal. Every time I read this it hurts. I can't stand it that he shuts the portal and refuses the adventure. I hate that moment. The goats wail inside me every time.

My breath is tight and shallow, my feet warm in the May sunlight.

I write:

Why do I hate that?

If I know anything, it's that it has to be a projection. *I* shut the portal up, fearful. I'm the one. What big adventure, what ship in full sail am I closing the door on?

What's there?

I *want* that, I want that ship and adventure. What story is in the way?

It's too late.

I don't know where that portal is.

I'm not big enough.

I can't ask for that adventure.

What happens when I believe that?

I feel sad, small, scared, the familiar feeling of needing to stay under the radar. I think it's too late—I'm too old—don't have the money, don't know where it is, won't step up to it, shouldn't compete, need to be careful, take it slow, not ask for the big stuff, don't even let on that the big stuff is there. Whoo.

Who would I be without this story, that I can't ask for that adventure?

Thrilled. Expectant. Calm. Available to see what appears.

Turnaround: *I can ask for that adventure.*

Of course I can. I do want it—and the universe has told me to ask for horses.

After this bit of work, I feel clearer. It isn't really Auberon's failure that bothers me, it's mine, and having looked at it, I relax. The pear tree outside my tall windows is a field of snowy blossoms, a rodeo of light. I open my computer, and just for fun do a search for "Tall ship Atlantic crossing."

The first hit comes up. "Sail from Europe to South America, 44 days." I click through, see a picture of a tall ship in full white-winged sail.

"Might as well see."

I send off a question: "I am sixty-two years old; is that a problem?"

The office in Holland writes back in a minute. "If you are fit, age is not a problem, but if you want to do this, you should reserve a berth now, as one of the legs of the trip is almost full. You can have two weeks to confirm."

"Yes, please. Hold a berth. I'll see what I can do."

I consult with my eighty-six-year-old mother. "Are you okay with me being at sea for six weeks? No internet, no phone?"

"Go, go!" she says.

I wire a pile of Euros to a bank in Rotterdam.

Four months from now I hope to step off a dock in the Canary Islands onto the deck of *Bark Europa*. I am sick of the black bird stage of this story. Maybe if I get onto an actual, living ship with white canvas sails, I'll find the happy ending to my dream.

THREE LIVES – *Past Life Regression*

June 2, 2016
62 years old

About a month after this step toward setting sail on a tall ship, I drive across town to a hypnotist's house. It hasn't been easy to find a hypnotist who admits to doing past life regressions. Most hypnosis websites focus on quitting smoking or overeating. I understand their reluctance—in our part of the world, the idea of reincarnation tends to make people roll their eyes.

A dozen years ago, I started to wonder whether I believed in reincarnation or not. I decided I didn't have enough evidence either way, so I went to the library and got out a stack of books. Most of the books could have been hogwash, nothing particularly verifiable. But one was different: *Life before Life*, about Ian Stevenson and his team from Duke University. His researchers interviewed hundreds of children under five who reported remembering a previous life, and then investigated to see whether their memories checked out, and couldn't have been acquired through "normal" means. Their research came out of a mindset that I like: *Could this be true?* How do we find out? What if we didn't reject this idea out of hand? His findings were solid enough to tip me over into a tentative yes, though I still hold the belief lightly. Standing here on the hypnotist's porch, I am curious. Ready to go somewhere new.

He opens the door—bearded, alert, seems normal enough. We sit in his red-and-black living room, with a Buddha glowing in the corner.

"I want to know if Will and I have known each other before. And I want some big-picture feel for my life: What am I trying to learn in this lifetime? What kind of person am I?"

He explains how he works and that I can wake up any time I want. It all makes sense. I lie back in a comfortable recliner, and he sets up the recorder.

First, he leads me through a conscious, pleasant memory,

with as much sensory detail as I can recall. I choose a day in Argenta, by Kootenay Lake. It's right there: the smell of balm-of-Gilead trees, the blue-silver shine of the lake, the curling sound of the rocks rubbing against each other on the shore. I tell it as it comes clear.

"That's a lot like what we're going to do," he says. "It's just a deeper memory, and it's going to be pleasant. We're going to go into three different lives, and we'll start each one by looking down at your feet. You'll be able to look up at the rest of your body from there, and you'll have a sense of the time, your age, what kind of person you are. We'll visit three moments in each life—the first one, however old you are, then middle life, then your death. At the death you'll get to have a chance to feel over the whole of that life, and what you learned."

The feet of the first person are barefoot, hardened, brown. I am a young woman, somewhere in the English countryside—a farmwife. Perhaps six or eight hundred years ago. I have a tall quiet husband, kind and skillful with our sheep and animals. We live in a small cottage, and a couple of old people live with us. I have the sense of an open, mostly outdoor life, hard work, loss and grief—no children—but a dear, loving husband. The overriding flavor at the moment of my death is gratitude and love for him.

The next person has shoes on: little black buttoned boots. I can hear the clop of horses' hooves on a street outside. It amazes me—again—how a whole world begins to unfold, starting from tiny clues. The feeling of a place and time blossoms through as I relax and watch and listen.

This person feels constricted, starting with the boots. I am a child, eight or ten years old, in a world of propriety and prosperity. Maybe Boston? Somewhere around 1880? I rebel against the constrictions, and as an adult woman I am a suffragist. Not well known, but friends with some of the well-known women, and with a sense of purpose and pleasure in the work. I live to be old, well into the twentieth century, can celebrate the passage of the Nineteenth Amendment. I stay single and amused all my life.

No one in these two experiences had reminded me in any way of Will, so in my third descent I send a strong intention to be taken somewhere that he was. This is why I'd driven over here to be hypnotized, after all.

It is a harder lifetime to find, in some way. Longer ago, further away, deeper in. And more of a story.

My feet are dark and dusty, in worn leather sandals. The air is hot, dry, loud: a market, a cacophony of saddlebags, rugs, dust, spice, dogs, people yelling, camels braying. I wear a grimy dirt-colored tunic. I am a young, resentful man about eighteen years old, a laborer in a camel caravan. We are unloading camels in the chaos. I watch the man who is buying from us—dressed in glowing soft fabrics, purple and red. I want to be him. I want that. I am ashamed to be poor and dirty, to be no one.

In the next scene, I am in my thirties, and I have become a merchant. I am part owner of the caravan. My coat is beautifully sewn and embroidered. We have stopped for the night in a town in Central Asia, Kabul or Kashgar, somewhere along the road between China and Persia. The person I know in this lifetime as Will is another part owner of the caravan, and we are friends. We've walked this trek through the desert before.

I have come into the city alone, to meet someone.

I don't know what he looks like or how to find him, but I've been instructed to go to the central square. I stand there in the late afternoon sunlight. The dome of a beautiful blue mosque towers over the square. The air is hot, quiet, dry. No one is waiting for me. Old men in long beards, drinking tea in teahouses around the square, stare at me. Bright birds in cages hang from doorways. I don't know what to do. Should I go back to the caravan?

This moment has a strange suspension to it, an intensity, like the moment in *Ask for Horses* when the bird-girl asks me if I think the peddlers will give me a gift. As if the world is waiting to see what I will do.

I finally sit down at a tile-covered table and order a glass of tea. In a few minutes, a man comes over and sits down across from me. It's him: the one I'm supposed to meet. He is a teacher, a spiritual or esoteric teacher, older than I am, with a beard and dark eyes. Those eyes change me; I am seen. It's all it takes. I'm his.

I don't even go back to the caravan to say goodbye. I send a message back with a boy, telling "Will" that he can have my share of all our trade goods and camels, everything. He'll be twice as rich as he was.

The last scene, at my death, is in a cave, surrounded by my students, with butter lamps flickering in the dark. I have become the teacher. I'm very conscious—more than I am in this current waking lifetime.

**

The hypnotist summons me back to wakefulness. I lie in his chair for fifteen minutes letting the experience settle, like light settling on the sandy bottom of a lake, while he puts the recording onto a CD. I feel as rested and clear as if I have been meditating for hours.

I wake the day after this session, crying. Slow, grateful tears like warm rain. "Why didn't I do this sooner?" I ask the air.

I make tea, open my journal, and sit in my red chair looking into the green branches of the tree. The warm teacup mirrors some glow inside me. That hypnosis session enlarged me. I can't remember ever being so relaxed. I don't know whether I really visited past lifetimes, though. It's possible, but I don't think so. It just wasn't odd or unfamiliar enough, somehow. It felt more like guided meditation—guided by some part of me—somewhere between waking life and dream. Hypnosis sent me into a deep, intuitive storytelling state.

I love all three stories, the last one especially.

The first one, the barefoot farmwife, felt strangely blessed, even while it was such hard work. It was earthen. I was tended, loved. The second one, so much more recent, so literate and busy, had a creative, wry, rebellious flavor, and was satisfying in an entirely different way from the farmwife. I feel richer, livelier, for having touched down inside those versions of myself, like a black-and-white drawing that has been partly colored in.

I drink my green tea and pat my sock-footed toes on the carpet. The third lifetime, the one I really went to the hypnotist to get, had other gifts altogether. For one thing, I was more awake in that one—by the end—than I am now. That's cool. And unexpected.

My tentative theory of reincarnation includes the notion that we become more awake as we go through lives. But according to this past-life story, not necessarily! And here I'm reminded that I know more or less nothing about how it all works. Death, rebirth, the survival of the soul: it's good to ask the questions, but crucial *not* to think we've got the answers. The best I can hope for is a model of reality that feels life-giving—that is merciful, spacious, and evolutionary. Having reincarnation in my model suits me because it allows for many chances to learn. In this story, the possibility that I was more evolved a thousand years ago just serves to remind me that my model is only a sketch on the wind.

Of course, this story can't tell us much about how reincarnation actually works, because I probably wasn't truly visiting another life. It begs to be read as a dream, however. Is it showing me some undeveloped potential? Hinting that I *could* be far more conscious in this lifetime than I am now? I wonder. More, I hope, will be revealed about that. But what most intrigues me about that Central Asian story is the moment of shift, standing in the quiet city square: the decision, the willingness to entirely alter the course of my life.

I breathe into the memory of that shift, the strange freedom of it.

The breeze through my open window smells like sap rising, like leaves opening, like violets and dirt. It is good to know that somewhere inside me is a character with enough courage and hunger for God—for the mystery—to leap right out into the unknown. I think of my sister Kathryn's favorite quote, from the Sufi story "The Parliament of the Birds":

You must have lions' hearts to go by that way,
it is not short and its seas are deep;
you will walk it long in wonder,
sometimes smiling, sometimes weeping.

Was this session any help at all with my problem? Did I learn anything about Will?

Not sure. It's interesting that I cast him as a friend, not a lover, in this tale. I'm glad I gave him a lot of camels when I left. But I don't know a lot more about how to walk forward in this moment. Still, the whole endeavor seems to have loosened the grip of my grief. I feel—what?—better. It is like being reminded that I'm a cell in some great being, that I'm part of something that is alive—ongoing—aware—and much much bigger than "me."

I am right between laughing and crying. Some of each. I put

down teacup, journal, pen; slide into my clogs; run down the stairs and out into the sunlight, headed for the river.

WHY AM I GOING THROUGH ALL THIS? – *Dream*

June 5, 2016
62 years old

I'm standing in a crowd of thirty or forty people, all looking at me.

I ask: "Why am I going through all this?"

An answer appears, written on the ground: *You couldn't live that way anymore.*

I answer, "I had a dream!"

I ask some people in the crowd, all of whom know me, and seem eager to speak.

A little girl with a bright face says, "Because you want to see the queen!"

An old bearded man, my teacher from the past life story in Central Asia, says, "Because you are hungry to learn."

I sense that any one of the people here would have an answer, each one different. There's a feeling of mystery, of waking up.

WHY AM I GOING THROUGH ALL THIS? – *Reflection*

My venture into hypnosis, looking for clues to my current grief, did help.

But the most valuable bit of help did not relate to Will at all. It is the moment in the Central Asian city square when I don't know what to do. The most striking minutes of the whole hypnosis session are the ones I spend standing in the late afternoon sunlight, when the person I expect to meet is not there. I tell the hypnotist, as I narrate what's happening:

"There's a sense of waiting—of people all around the square watching."

I feel the hot silence of the square, the pigeons, the great blue mosque, the bearded old men in red coats. Something about the way they are watching makes me suddenly laugh.

"I probably know them all!"

He laughs as well.

"It feels like *my life* is watching, the important witnesses are here."

The people sitting around that Central Asian square may look like a cluster of old men, but that is a disguise: I think they are my inner witnesses and helpers, the important figures of my dreams and psyche. They are watching to see whether I will go back to the camel caravan or step onto the crazy path of spiritual discipleship—a choice that in some way is alive inside me right now. Having been drawn together in my past-life adventure, they are primed to show up three days later in this short dream.

What I love about this assembly in the dream is that each person is ready to give a different answer to my question: there are *dozens* of reasons that I am going through all this. All the parts of my once-and-future self want to walk me through this grief, just as, in the hypnosis session, they wanted me to sit down at a tiled table in the shade of a blue mosque, and wait.

This seems clear both inside the dream and when I wake up. It doesn't seem coded or symbolic in the way of most dreams but a summoning of the clan, a straightforward gathering to help me stay the course. The pain is walking me across a bridge into a different way of living my life. All right. I take heart. I do.

But what does this mean:

You couldn't live that way anymore.

What way would that be, exactly?

CHOOSING CLOTHES FOR THE END OF THE WORLD – *Dream*

September 14, 2016
63 years old

It's the end times. The world is emptying out; maybe we've run out of food. I'm with a group of people at a big house on a cliff overlooking water, a river or an ocean. My daughters are around, younger than they are now.

The house belongs to Jack. He has a powerful weapon, a ray gun that looks like a piece of dried meat, a pepperoni stick. Squatters are staying in some of the bedrooms, living there without his consent. A couple walks out of a bedroom. The man looks at Jack and says, "I'm not afraid of your ray gun," and Jack shoots him with it. He hangs in the air, paralyzed, but alive inside. It's awful. It's a terrible power, and Jack doesn't use it indiscriminately, but it's enough to make everybody obey him.

He tells us it's time to get going. We mill around outside in the sunlight. We're going to drive down the cliffside to the water. That's where it's all going to end. I overhear, but don't really believe, a rumor that we might set up a farm and start over.

I go inside to look for clothes before we go. There are rooms full of clothes. I am wearing a soft, colorful silk skirt and find a top that goes with it—a pretty tunic. I put it on and then start to wonder: What is actually going to happen? If we are going to farm, these aren't the right clothes. I should wear jeans for that. But I don't think we are. I think we're going to all die or be killed.

There's such a big, strange, mysterious feeling to all this. Jack's gun and his humorlessness with it are icky and intense. I wonder, does the ray effect wear off, or do these people just die because they can't eat or poop?

CHOOSING CLOTHES FOR THE END OF THE WORLD — *Reflection*

> *The shadow personifies everything that the subject refuses to acknowledge about himself.*
> —Carl Jung

I carry this dream around in my body, startled, mystified: Why is it set in such a *huge* frame, with the sense of an entire civilization powering down?

I'm about to leave for my adventure in a couple of weeks. I feel more grounded about Will and have accepted that we won't get back together—but nothing about any of that feels like the end of the world. So where is that apocalyptic energy coming from?

Nick and Chena and I meet for dream group at their office. It's only the three of us. We eat mushroom soup and oranges and open a bottle of red wine. The smell of sawdust and rain and wine fills their back room.

We all tell a dream while we are eating. Mine is so big that we decide to tackle it first.

Nick asks, "What was your feeling when you woke up?"

"Awe-struck. High stakes. Horror about Jack's ray gun. He used it to make us all do what he wanted. But when I woke up I was mostly just blown away. The end of the world. Science-fiction."

"What was the moment of most intensity?" Chena asks.

"That moment when Jack froze the guy and suspended him in mid-air. It was like something out of a Harry Potter movie. A spell. Like *petrificus totalis*."

"Does anything in your waking life feel like that?"

"No . . . not really. Except for the way Jack used to freeze people out of his life. Like he never spoke again to our good friends in Hawaii once he found out they smoked pot. I hated that harshness, cutting people off."

I think about the ray gun.

"It looks a little like a dried-up penis, with a bent end. And it's a stick of dried meat—a Slim Jim, like you buy at a gas station. A slim jim is also a locksmith tool, with a bent tip. But a slim jim is a tool for unlocking a car, not for freezing things up. I'm not sure what that's about. Maybe there's something helpful about that weapon that I'm not seeing."

We sip wine. Traffic sizzles along the rainy, dark street outside.

"Ah. I'm seeing something about masculinity," I say. "A discomfort with my own masculine energy. There's that ray gun that looks like a penis. And the clothes. The jeans I don't want to wear are masculine, and the pretty soft clothes are feminine."

I lean back and look up at the ceiling.

"In the dream, I do not believe we are going to start a farm. I'm ready for it all to end. But I wonder about that. Why? Why don't I consider that we might start over?"

Nick says, "If this were my dream, I would look again at the clothes. If there's *any* chance of starting over, it would be worth wearing the jeans. Right? Why not wear some less comfortable clothes for a few hours? At worst, I die in them. At best, I'm ready for the new life. So what is that choice even about?"

"Yeah, you're right, that's what I'm wondering. It's weird," I said. "Why *am* I so passive? I'm just more comfortable in the pretty clothes."

"Yes," Chena says. "If this were my dream, it would be asking me if I would rather die than change. Because I don't want to be uncomfortable. And the same thing with the ray gun. Could this be in my shadow? Do I always want to be the nice guy? What if the dream is suggesting that it's time to be the mean guy? Time to get outside my comfort zone?" She looks at me. "What do you think?"

"Yes yes yes! That ray gun must be in my shadow, because I can't stand it. What if the dream wants me to try being harsh and cold—and *tough*, like the jeans are tough? What if that slim jim will *unlock* something?" I laugh.

Hm. I feel an "aha!"—but is the dream telling me to be harsh and tough with Will? No way. We're friends. It's got to be something else.

"So, bumper sticker?" Nick asks.

"Put on the tough pants," I say.

We clean up and head out into the darkness, nourished with wine and mystery.

A couple of weeks later Will drives me to the airport, kisses me goodbye. "I'm so proud of you," he says. "I don't know anyone else who would take on an adventure like this."

I look at him, aware of all that we've been through, and how much we love each other still. I push through the glass airport doors buoyant and eager for my trip, but not quite free.

***

I have some clues, now, about why the dream came on apocalyptic wings. First, to shine a harsh light on some choices I had to make. I had to see that *everything* in my recovery was riding on my willingness to be uncomfortable, to put on the hard pants. I had glimpsed this truth, but not really absorbed it, at the time I pushed through the airport doors.

And there are other ways to read this dream. What if it is a story for all of us right now on our planet? It could be that we collectively face a similar choice. Maybe the stakes of our passivity really are that high. Would humanity as a whole—like me in the dream—rather die than change?

HAWKEYE

Why has this been so hard for her?

Well, she'd made a deal.
She traded her need for power, risk, and real conversations, for comfort and shelter.
She spent so much that she can't believe it didn't work.

That was the witch. The part of her who worked sideways, worked underground, made deals she wasn't aware of.

She burned the witch eventually.

But only because we told her to!
Ah.
You couldn't live that way anymore.
She doesn't know what we meant.
No, but she will.

WHAT *DID* THEY MEAN?

Years later, I'm still wondering exactly what that writing on the ground in my dream meant. *You couldn't live that way anymore?*

What way?

Since the witch in the *Pyre* dream appears to represent the way I couldn't live anymore, let's look at her.

A witch has plenty of magical power, but her community doesn't trust her. She has no official status. The villagers may depend on her secret knowledge, but they visit her on the sly. She is not loved or known, and her powers are not granted free, full play. She has the frustrated energy of the sled dog pulling her skateboard around the backyard. *Thwarted* is the exact word. And she is vulnerable too! Unprotected. The villagers might burn her up (though in this case she does it herself).

A queen, on the other hand, is beloved and celebrated. Flags, music, sunlight, the whole deal. Her people depend openly on her ability to think straight and govern. She is like one of the dogs on the team racing through the snow with the serum. She might even be Togo, the lead dog on the toughest stretch of the run. Her powers are not only permitted but essential.

The witch lives in the shadows, and the queen has arisen from them, whole.

My psyche, my committee of characters within and without, was evidently done playing small, being frustrated, settling for less than full-out play. I had outgrown my box—though I didn't want to leave it! I felt safe in there, I fought to stay in it, to stay in the circle of Will's arms. That desire turned out not to be the strongest force inside me, however. I was being taught, changed, enlarged, by some force inside me that wanted to see the queen, that wanted to run through the snow, that could hear the far-off sound of hoofbeats.

ELEVEN
In which I sail across the ocean

BARK EUROPA

September–November 2016
63 years old

In Tenerife, a European town in the Canary Isles off the coast
of Africa, I amble down a steep sunny street from my hostel
to the docks to get my first look at *Europa*. Tall masts rocking,
sails wrapped tight, she is asleep. My heart lifts, as if wind has
filled it. Holy cow.

This flower of a ship was built in 1911 in Hamburg. For
decades she served as a lightship in the Elbe River, and in 1994
was re-rigged as a three-masted barque in Amsterdam. Now a
sail training ship registered in the Netherlands, she is 184 feet
long and only twenty-four feet wide, a narrow blade of steel
and wood. She carries twenty-six sails, from the flying jib at
the bow to the gaff topsail at the stern. I've drawn a picture of
her in my journal, naming all the sails. I can't wait to go aboard.

The next day, I walk down the same steep street wearing my
backpack. Here we go!

I hoist my pack up the gangway, passing it to a tan, strong girl
with wild hair, part of the crew. I jump down onto the wooden
deck, weaving between packs, cases of lettuce and massive coils
of rope (soon to be known as line). The other travelers show
up and dump their packs. All told, when we embark, there are
fifty of us. Nineteen paid crew and thirty-one who have paid
our Euros to learn to sail; we are the "voyage crew." Fifteen
women and thirty-five men, from twelve countries. We'll be
together for six weeks before we get to Montevideo, sailing in
all about 4,000 nautical miles.

It is a Dutch ship culture, which means friendly, not military.
There are no uniforms and no shouted orders. The captain, tall
and wide and blond, wears shorts and flip-flops. He expects
excellence from his crew, and they are amazing, scrambling
around in the rigging, teaching us how the ship works, constantly painting and repairing. Every night, the captain unrolls

the big charts and shows us where we are, what our heading has been, how far we've come that day. The working language is English, thank god.

The voyage crew is divided into watches, Red, Blue, and White; I'm on Red. We take turns on the foredeck, watching for floating containers, fishnets, whales. Or on the poopdeck, at the back, nudging the big wooden steering wheel this way and that, trying to keep the ship on the course assigned to us by the captain. We keep our eyes not on the big deck compass but on a waterproof iPad that shows the course reading. 180 degrees, much of the time. Straight south.

Otherwise we eat, nap, practice knots, talk to crewmates, play pranks on each other, haul on line to raise or lower sail: *Two, six, HEAVE!*

Except when asleep, I live on deck. I begin to dread returning to a world of houses. It is hard to imagine living shut away from the wind and air.

Sometimes I take the helm at night. Steering the ship through the dark ocean, I'm barely able to stay in my body, it is so ridiculous and amazing. Like finding myself on the deck of the *Dawn Treader*, sailing for the edge of the world. All sails set and full. The ninety-foot mainmast towering and dipping as we plunge forward. Green sparkles of light bursting in our wake.

GIVING IT TO THE OCEAN

September–November 2016

Marina, a social worker from Switzerland, sits with me on a bench on the deck peeling potatoes. Sun on the backs of our necks and hands. Smell of turpentine. Sails full, in a steady wind; ship well heeled over, on the same heading — 190 — that we've been on for some days. I tell Marina that even inside the joy of this adventure, I feel a lingering stab from my breakup with Will, and that I came to give it to the ocean.

When the potatoes are finished, I go stand on the foredeck, my favorite place, right under the mainsail. The warm deck boards are nice to my bare feet. The sail is as big as the wall of a house, and the canvas heavy enough to hoist a car. *Working cloth,* I think. I grab the bottom of it, and the wind tugs. I take a breath, loving the immense sail, the long wooden yards like polished tree trunks, all this line, wood and knots and paint — the sturdiness, straight-aheadness, density, power, presence; the non-digital, very analog, *reality* of it. I breathe out, still holding the living, heavy canvas. The blue ocean splashes itself onto the deck. A shining flock of tiny things — flying fish — darts out of the sea and back in, like spray. I feel like a dog with its head out the window. The moment is some kind of mortal being, a wild creature made of light and water and wind and canvas.

***

The Boil
I have a bad boil on my butt, which the ship's doctor, Marie, has been lancing.

"Maybe it's time to take antibiotics?" I suggest.

We've been treating this a few days and it hurts like a hot needle.

"No," she says. "Maybe I can inject an anesthetic, and try to get it cleaned out — because it hurts so much that I can't really squeeze it well enough."

"Okay," I say.

I cry silently into the blue flannel sheets on my little bunk as she tries to clean it out.

"Sorry, sorry."

In between treatments, I think about the boil as if it were a dream. I have some old raw hurt, trying to come to the surface to be healed. But it's not a clean eruption; it's a painful, messy process, putting me through a lot of sharp pain. It could be a metaphor for the whole long breakup thing with Will or even my long and early distress with my dad. Something *coming to a boil.*

After midnight, I sit in the deckhouse with Marina and her sister Sabra, waiting for our turn on watch. I tell them about the boil and how an old hurt seems to be coming to the surface.

"What I see now," I tell Marina, "is how much of my pain came from telling myself I was okay with things that I was truly not okay with. Denial! Repression! I am really good at it. But I have got to learn to tell myself the truth."

"I think you are learning it," she says.

Her sister nods. The warm, venerable smell of bread baking rises from below deck.

***

The Suitcase

A week later . . . I'm on deck, early morning, staring into whiteness. Marie, the doctor, comes and stands next to me. The boil is finally clean and we don't have to spend every afternoon gritting our teeth together. We're still friends.

The journey is almost over. In a couple of days we'll reach Montevideo, where the ship will go on without me to Antarctica. We're sailing in the Falkland Current now. The water is seventeen degrees; at midnight it was twenty, so it has dropped three degrees. This has caused the fog. It's wonderful, silent and spooky—very *Dawn Treadery*—gliding through the white world, in a calm sea. A faint petroleum smell—some tanker nearby?

I smile at Marie. She is so pretty. I used to look like that. Oh well. I did something amazing, coming on this adventure. I'm more or less twice as old the other women on the ship. I'm sorry this wonderful time is ending, but it has helped me. I gave my pain to the ocean, and I can feel what happened to it. I wanted the salt water to swallow it, but no. The ocean gave it back to me in a suitcase. And all those sunny, windy, stormy nautical miles—plus the boil—have strengthened me. I no longer have to get rid of my pain. It still hurts, but I am bigger than it is. I survived the lancing of my boil, and I am strong enough to carry that suitcase.

We keep sailing into nothing. My hair is damp with cloud.

HAWKEYE

Wasn't that fun?
She needed that, to be still and move at the same time.
To look at waves, at sky and water, day after day.

It was medicine for all of us.
Oh, it was for sure. Being a frigatebird!
Being a sail!
Wowzer!

TWELVE
In which I get a new coat

USING THE RAY GUN

I'm sad to step off the ship in Uruguay; I love this windy, straightforward, salt-smelling, dolphin-blessed, canvas-driven life. A short, friendly English teacher, Italian by birth, hosts me for a few days in Montevideo (through the travel service Servas). She takes me to a Tibetan sound healing, which helps me to stop reeling from the terrible news of the Trump election. I slowly get my land legs and land mind back. I am thinner, tanner, tougher than when I left home. The ocean has become a presence in my body which I will always miss, like a sister.

Back in Oregon, it finally dawns on me that while Will wants to be my friend, I don't want to be his. It's too hard on me. I also discover that I am in possession, figuratively speaking, of the ray gun from the *End of the World* dream. And I'm ready to use it.

I move my studio out of his house, give back his key, and stop talking to him.

Who knew there was a healthy place in me for humorless distancing?

He is stunned.

I feel a lot better. The windows in my head stop rattling.

SHRAPNEL

It is a giant relief to have cut Will out of my life—but dammit, something is still wrong. I have a sharp pain in my upper right chest. A buried bit of shrapnel. I just can't shake the fact that he's chosen someone else.

So I get a dream about jealousy.

BARBARA IS JEALOUS OF MY PRETTY COAT — *Dream*

March 26, 2017

I come across a beautiful dark coat with orange embroidery and try it on.

My sister Barbara is watching. She's jealous.

I suggest she find a garment she likes as much.

She is dismissive: "I could never afford something like that."

"The only reason I can afford it is . . ." I pause to recall how I actually did afford it, and my answer surprises me. ". . . I inherited it."

BARBARA IS JEALOUS OF MY PRETTY COAT
— *Reflection*

I was two years old when my sister Barbara was born. I was shocked when she showed up—and she was more shocked to find me already there. I stood in her way, the oldest child, already beloved. She was mad. We fought like rats. She never could catch up, and the harder and hotter she fought, the cooler and smarter I acted. I said that I didn't understand her—her wild and angry restless energy—but in fact I was distancing from her. I was still trying to win, to look good, to be the rational character in the scene.

It was true that I didn't understand her; I didn't want to. I was scared of getting too close to her pain. Until this year, and this breakup, I really didn't know what a sharp stone jealousy is. The panic of unworthiness, the shame of not being the One: give me a break. Who would want to feel that? Who would lean into a sister's pain, when you started out as the cause of her distress? Not me, no.

It's not like we were estranged. For most of our lives, until she died at fifty-five, we were friends. But in some way, sandpaper friends. Still grit under the skin somewhere. When my sisters died, I built a shrine for Kathryn, with some of her art and quotes, a picture of the two of us, and a nesting felted golden bird. But I never made one for Barbara—it just didn't come.

Sitting in my red chair, realizing Barbara carried something like this jealous feeling, I am hammered with compassion for her—she felt like *this?*—oh god—my body is alive, heavy, hot, prickly, full of a storming energy. The Berlin Wall is crumbling inside me. I've lived with this barricade and not wanted to see it, all my life.

And bam, I understand something about Will. He is behaving exactly as I did most of my life. Backing away from pain, from the heavy emotion, making himself feel (and look) rational by comparison. I took a huge emotional hit from our breakup, while he "moved on" as if it were no big deal. Why?

Now I know.

I write, with tears falling on the words, "I forgive him. I get it. I couldn't take down that wall either. *I couldn't do it*—it was life threatening."

I feel kindled. Seeing what I couldn't see before makes me aware, again, that we only ever take in the slenderest slice of reality. I can feel the nudging presence of a tremendous life force, "a holy energy that fills the universe, playing like lightning," as the fourteenth-century mystic Jan van Ruysbroek put it.

A week later, as the bombs of awareness are still going off, it seems possible that the breakup is the best thing that ever happened to me. Because it has exposed such deep, dark, difficult stuff. The painful boil got opened. If I squint, I can start to see the whole thing as a play. And what do you know?!—a play is *exactly* that mysterious thing that Will talked about in his jet-boat-explosion dream, *a fictional tour one can also go on.*

My *Pyre* dream also called attention to itself as a play, with its three-act form, and references to *Lear* and *H.M.S. Pinafore.* The whole drama was a big cycle that was known to some much larger part of me, in grave detail, far in advance. Part of the purpose of the play was, I now see, to heal this old thing with Barbara.

Suddenly I find—almost seven years after her death—that I am ready to make a shrine for her. I build it, paint it, glue a miniature antique pickup truck with the words "Content Farm" on top, set it beside the one I'd made for Kathryn. I finally have both sisters tucked together inside me. No more blockades.

Worth the price of admission. What a dream. The grass-field smell of her farm, with clean baby goats and green onions, blows through my heart.

But then I come back to this dream as I am writing this book, and a whole new layer blazes out. The beautiful coat—the jealous sibling—it's a story from the Bible. How did I miss that?

Well, I got so much from the first run at the dream that I

didn't need to look further. But this time through it says: "I am an old tale. Of jealous siblings, of betrayal and redemption. *And* I am a story of how dreams saved an entire people from famine." By invoking the Bible story of Joseph and his coat of many colors, the dream-writers give this dream a heavy, deep hum. It reverberates down into my body, into the many tones and songs of the word *inheritance*.

This beautiful coat was *handed down* to me. Not just from my parents, who taught me my Quaker, literate, repressed way of being in the world, but all the way down, from Joseph and his people. The orange embroidery on the dark background is a symbol of storytelling—the creative embroidery that brings the essence of old tales to life. And it also recalls flames, bright trails of fire against the darkness.

This coat could be a symbol of my book. Maybe I'm trying on a storytelling garment that calls up all the longings and losses we've inherited from those ancestors on whose shoulders we stand—including Joseph, whose skill as a dreamworker and dreamer was given so much weight by the tribes whose stories became our Old Testament.

Long, long ago, back in the days of the desert, we trusted dreams to help keep us alive. What if we did that again? What if my vision of a dream-reliant society is not foolishness but a dark, flame-embroidered possibility—an actual mantle, handed down from the oldest times, that I can wear for a few years while it is my turn? A coat that I can pass down to those who come after me?

DROWNING CAR – *Dream*

April 21, 2017
63 years old

I'm driving my blue Prius through the countryside, up and down hills. I drive down a big hill—with my eyes closed. I coast mindlessly along and suddenly *I've driven into the ocean.* The tide is up, the ocean is here, holy shit we're going down, the car is full of water, I'm going to die.

"Here it is," I say. The moment of my death is here. I am not afraid but it is so intense.

Finally I start to wonder if I can get out.

"Unbuckle the seatbelt!" I keep telling myself, and I finally do. After that the next step is not swimming out the window but peeling off blankets, pushing back the covers. I push them back and I'm out, prepared for a hard swim back to land, but my feet touch bottom. It's only a few feet deep. My eyes open, it's sunny, I walk to shore. I look back and realize the car is floating.

Whoa! I thought—I was sure!—I'd lost everything. But I'm alive. Maybe I can even salvage my car? I go back out and pull it in. It comes easily, floats easily. I get it to shore and it's even easy to pull up onto the sand. Amazing.

There's a garage here, a little way up the road. A mechanic is there on the beach, and I take the car over to him. "It was in the salt water. Is there any way you can salvage it?"

The car is now white. All the traces of blue paint are gone. There are some faint lines of writing on it—black, and a little red. It's a slightly different style too. Flatter.

He looks at the car, inside it, under the hood, and says, "Sure, I can clean this up while you take a nap."

I wake up staggered.

A big, gusty, unfamiliar space has opened in my chest.

Sunlight flickers through pear blossoms onto my hands and blankets, as I remember my way through the dream. *So . . . they want me to know it's all being taken care of. That from here on it gets easier. But they also want me to almost die. Wow.*

Two feelings stay with me as I carry this dream around with me: the knife-blade presence of my death and the ease of everything after I push back the covers.

I take it to dream group.

" 'Pushing back the covers' means a few things," I say. "Getting out of Will's bed."

Sigh. "Pushing off the coverings that hide my own light. And waking up to a new day."

Deep breath.

Nick remembers our conversation about *Choosing Clothes for the End of the World.* "If this were my dream," he says, "here is this passive thing again! I have to turn a corner inside myself. Instead of just accepting my death, I have to wonder: *Maybe I can get out?*"

I feel the thump of recognition in my gut as he says this. Yes. I have to take action in my own favor. *I have to unbuckle the seatbelt.*

There's another thing.

After being underwater, my blue Prius is flatter, white, with tiny red and black lines of print on it, like the sponsorship logos on a race car.

What do you know!—It's my journal again! Having appeared in other dreams as a log, a birchbark torch, and a brick-making factory, it is now a small flat fast car.

We all feel the click.

"My journal this month is written partly in red ink," I tell them, noting the red print on the car.

A few days later, the eve of May Day, I am going to sleep

and having a hard time once again—what the hell!!— navigating my pain. I ask my Inner Wise Self for help.

"It's not a puzzle to be solved," she says.

"It's not? It sure feels like it," I say. "So what is it?"

"A window to be opened."

Suddenly there it is: the window, an open window, and outside of it, snow mountains. Somewhere like Switzerland. A fresh, living air. It's wonderful, the sense of air and opening, the big world out there, the aliveness and beauty. What a difference between it and the world I am falling asleep in. And intense: almost too intense to revisit next morning in my meditation.

In that moment I see or remember that "I" am not a real or solid thing. I'm a movement, a murmuration, a fluid space like water—not an "I" that things happen to, things that I get to take personally or seriously. Not a solid target. That is such a relief. And very much the easeful flavor of the end of this drowning car dream. I recall Tara Brach saying that "the path of awakening is simply a process of wakeful, profound relaxing." This dream, in the end, takes me there. It's being taken care of.

AMBUCHI — *Dream*

May 1, 2017, nap
63 years old

I'm out in the woods with my friend Paula and her husband Harland. Paula invites me to go on an adventure to a remote place. She shows me a map of Asia, with a big empty unmapped space in the middle of it, around Siberia/Mongolia. It will take five nights to get there, and we'll stay five nights.

"Are those five nights on a train?" I ask.

"Yes."

We talk about beds, bedding, sheets, quilts. My sense of the room on the train gets nicer and nicer as we talk.

She says, "I'll work on the roommate thing."

"Boys are nice," I suggest.

She smiles and agrees. She says she'll work on that for me.

I'm touched and grateful that I can go on a great adventure like this, and I tell her, "I'm so glad I can go."

Then I drive down a curving steep dirt road, with two or three young women in the car. Talking, laughing, having fun. Down near the river, we drive over some big humps in the road. I get out and fall in the river. Now we have to go back so I can dry off. We walk back up, still laughing.

When we get back up, Paula tells me of a concept—*ambuchi*—which means "when you get something, you also get something else." The extra thing you get could be quite different.

She says, "For example, you get some in-laws, and along with them you get a memory of a lovely day you'd forgotten."

This concept has something to do with it being okay that I fell in the river. It is how I'll dry off, how I will recover.

AMBUCHI — *Reflection*

I wake up from the nap of this dream as rested as if I've spent a month in hibernation. I sit in my red armchair and watch the springy branches and curly leaves of the pear tree. Over the eight years I've lived in this room, the tree has shot up past the windows, so now I live in a treehouse, a bower of green light.

Exactly a year ago, I sat in this very chair and read the passage in *Little, Big* about the portal and the ship raising its sails offshore. During that year, in waking life, I did a past life regression, sailed on a tall ship across the Atlantic, stopped talking to Will, took an emotional-connection workshop from Raphael Cushnir, healed a life-long rift with my dead sister Barbara, and cried enough tears to fill a small well. In dreamland, I chose clothes for the end of the world, put on a storyteller's coat, and drove my car into the sea.

"Here I am, a year later, in the same red chair, watching sunlight in the leaves," I muse. "But I didn't shut the portal, like Auberon. I stepped through it onto the ship. And wow, do I feel better. It is incredible how much better I feel."

I laugh, feeling the sense of having traveled a long way in that *ambuchi* dream. A hummingbird flashes through the green mass of leaves, almost too quick to see. What a cool word. Where did it come from?

The dream tells me I am headed out into a great exploration—though I still have some drying off to do. But some blessing is afoot, a sweet change in the wind.

In waking life, I construct a costume. I buy a sparkly bridal tiara at the fabric store, and make a scepter out of a chair rung, ribbons, and a Nepalese *dorje*—a ritual thunderbolt. One evening, I try it all on: iridescent blue ball gown, crown, scepter. I smile at the fluffy-haired woman in the mirror. She smiles back, potent and beautiful. Great. I pack it all into a suitcase. Ready to rock and roll. It is a dance costume for the Dream Ball.

The closing event of the International Association for the Study of Dreams conference every year is the Dream Ball.

People come as characters from their dreams. It's pretty wild: a fish dances with an apple, Dorothy in her ruby slippers dances with a devil. At this year's conference in LA, I'm giving a presentation about my *Pyre* dream—and later that night I'm going to the dance as the queen.

One more fine thing: I am plunging into a year-long intensive with Raphael Cushnir. He is my kind of spiritual teacher. Clear as water, but also funny and ordinary—not a whiff of "wiser than you." By some miracle, he lives in Portland, and that makes it affordable; most of the thirteen people in this group live in other parts of the country. He calls it P4—*Presence, Purpose, Passion, and Power.* This space he is creating will be a place where I hope to push back the covers. Open the window. Ask for horses. Drink the black transformative liquid. All those things the dreams want me to do.

To prepare for our first retreat (just before the dream conference), Raphael asks us to write our life story in three sentences. It's hard to mash my life into a three-sentence narrative and finally I come up with:

There is no way to earn the love I need.
I've spent my life trying.
I give up.

When I read this aloud at our first P4 gathering, they laugh. One woman in the group asks me later: "Do you date?"

"No."

"You don't want to, or you just don't?"

"I just don't. I think I'm afraid to put myself out there. What if I fail again?"

My stomach hurts just talking to her about it. I've flunked so many times. My screwy twenties, let's not even think about that. Two burned-out marriages. This long strange heartbreak with Will. Urg.

I need help believing that I can do it differently—that I can show up as myself and tell the truth. Lo these many years I've tried to buy my way into safety and connection by attempting to be the person my lover can't live without. No good. Total fiasco in fact.

This dream gives me a word for coming at love from another direction.

Ambuchi.

Without my effort to squeeze myself into a lovable shape, I might know that my relaxed shape is lovable. And also loving. And that somehow love has been here all along, in every cell of the greenwood. That it burns in the pear-tree leaves and the hummingbird's flash, that it arrives like rain. It's here. We have nothing to do with its coming or leaving. If we stand outside with our faces up, like ferns, it fills us, sings in us, keeps us alive. We are part of it. But we don't earn it. We don't *make* it happen. All we can do is let go, and see. And maybe then even the past starts to shift, releasing a memory of a lovely day long forgotten. Maybe love begets more love.

The dream hints at some possibilities for my waking life. As that dream train rattles through the snow mountains of Central Asia, maybe the power of *ambuchi* will help me to open the door to my compartment to find . . . a tall man sitting on the bottom bunk, my roommate for the ride.

It will be a while, yet, before I meet that guy in waking life.

On our first walk by the river, Steve and I will ask each other what we've learned in our long relationship travels. As we pass under the bare, chilly cottonwoods, hands in our pockets, I'm ready to say one thing I've learned—the cost of not talking. If I can't tell the truth, if I don't feel safe enough in myself to know what I feel, if I can't trust someone with my ragged hungers and raw edges, there's no hope. Sooner or later the unsaid things will spill over into the soup and make everyone sick.

"You have to be willing to have courageous conversations," I say.

His face lights up.

What a good sign.

This walk is two years after the *Ambuchi* dream, but the dream helps me believe that it is coming.

HAWKEYE

That walk is coming. Her friend is coming.

She needs to dry off first.
She fell in the river—
but how lovely to see her laughing
as she walks back up! *Ambuchi* will help her
to stop crying, to dry off, to board that train
to the unmapped spot
in the center of Asia.

That is her favorite place,
the unexplored place on the map.
The space of what she doesn't know.
The mystery.
Isn't it great, to see her feeling this well,
packing her bags for that adventure?

THIRTEEN
In which a hole is made in my hand

THE BREAKFAST TABLE

The girls and I have lived with my father and his wife, Mary, for ten years now. My dad has turned himself into a refuge for us, utterly and kindly. The loss of my sisters hit him hard, and he is as tenderhearted as a leaf.

I've calmed down; my father has softened. I no longer feel the Moon Man chasing me, and I've long ago stopped running. My dad and I sit in the morning at the kitchen table. I hold my cup of jasmine tea and write in my journal; he drinks his first cup of coffee and reads the *New York Times* online. He is pretty deaf and we don't talk, but it's good to be together. It feels like home.

THE WITTA PRISONERS HAVE A NEW JOB – *Dream*

June 2, 2017
63 years old

The prisoners from the *Witta* dream are working in Venice as gondoliers. Their striped shirts are perfect; they already have the outfit for the job.

THE WITTA PRISONERS HAVE A NEW JOB — *Reflection*

This dream is a sweet little postcard. A dream of transfiguration, like the witch turning into the queen, or even — going all the way back to my winter in Denmark — a windmill being turned into an observatory. It's miraculous that the prisoners' striped uniforms, their markers of captivity, have outfitted them to ply the most graceful boats in the world along those luminous roads made of water.

It is generous of them to let me know how things turned out. I breathe in, breathe out. Some long-imprisoned parts of me are unshackled, lifting their oars.

THE DREAM CONFERENCE

My presentation for the dream conference is called *Dreaming My Way across the Ocean*. Fifty people have crammed into the long narrow room. I talk about the *Pyre* dream and the breakup, the burning witch, the black-winged bird and the Queen on her ship, the *Little, Big* portal and how I walked through that portal onto the deck of a tall ship. Bark Europa, in full sail, shines like a cloud on the pull-down screen, white-winged and incredible against the blue sky.

On another screen I show a quote from Jeremy Taylor:

> . . . *the unconscious element of our being from which the dreams spring is so much older, wiser, stronger, more creative, loving and reconciling than we even imagine...*

This is the point I want to emphasize, how wise and loving the forces are behind the dreams. I explain that the whole cycle of that Pyre dream was ignited by a current of intelligence that *wants* me to be whole, that wants me to be joyful, that wants me to step into the shoes of the Queen.

I end by saying, "And I'm going to the Dream Ball as the Queen!"

I laugh, and they do too.

That night, I have a dream.

THE SCARRED MAN AND THE SNOW LION — *Dream*

June 18, 2017
63 years old

I'm in remote, high backcountry like Alaska or western Montana, visiting a man with terrible scars on his face. He has built a log cabin. I am touched to be here; it feels good. I used to be involved with him. I haven't been here for several years.

He tells me that Nancy is here. I'm not jealous, though I think she is his girlfriend. Another woman is here, too.

The two women—now they are his sisters—take me on a drive into very high, mountainous country, like the country north of Yellowstone. They're in front and I'm in the back seat on the right.

One of them points and says, "Look!"

I see a flash of white—a bighorn sheep. Then another. And a snow leopard is stalking them: big heavy tail, white and blue mottled fur. It looks like a brushstroke, so alive and in motion. We swerve toward it, and suddenly one of the women shoots and kills it. As it falls, the cat pierces a single claw through the metal of the door and makes a hole in the side of my right hand.

I'm so shocked, seeing it lying dead in the road. All that moving, powerful life, gone. Empty.

We get back to the cabin, and tell the story. The kitchen is full of people. My aunt puts a gauze bandage on my wound, which bleeds like mad. We mill around getting ready to go into town, somewhere like Fairbanks.

The scarred man is apparently entitled to some compensation because of my wound.

"But," his sisters tell me, "we haven't been able to get any settlement for his earlier, terrible wounds—the ones that left the scars on his face. When we talk to the city officials, they agree to help, but after we leave they just shove the paperwork in a drawer. They never actually do anything."

"I've met officials like that," I say. "I get it."

The wound bleeds an amazing amount. The bandage is saturated, and the adhesive tape holding it is stringy with blood.

At the end of the dream, it's time to take the bandage off, and for all of us to go into town.

THE SCARRED MAN AND THE SNOW LION
— *Reflection*

The purpose of literature is to turn blood into ink.
T. S. Eliot

I wake in the vast white hotel bed to the dim clatter of Kirsten making coffee. I am still mostly in another place—far to the north and several years in the future. The awful sight of the dead snow leopard (which I thought of as a *snow lion*), the glow of golden logs in the scarred man's cabin, the chill of the wind in the mountains through which we drove, are more vivid than the hotel room. I can still feel the sticky bandage, red and sodden with blood, and hear the swirl of conversation in the cabin at the end of the dream as we prepare to leave for town. I lie in the growing light, smelling coffee, strangely and deeply relieved.

Something has happened.

It is over.

There've been plenty of clues that I am nearly done with my grief. The *Ambuchi* dream, the *Drowning Car* dream, the increasing jolts of random joy as I walk along the river, the way I stood up yesterday and gave my *Pyre* talk.

I listen to Kirsten puttering. It is done. Wow. Yay.

How did the dream do that? Loosen the last snarl, so that the net hung free?

It did three things, I discover, as I sit with it:

It gives me a *felt sense* of completion.

It allows me to understand Will in a new way.

It gives me my marching orders.

The first thing, the sense of completion, flows from the dream perspective of traveling several years ahead. It lets me feel all the recovery and peace that a few years of distance are going to provide. It is well beyond my waking ability to go out that far, but the dream can. It takes me to a place where my pain has left the room.

The second thing: It uses the symbol of red tape to explain something important about Will.

In the kitchen after the death of the snow lion, the scarred man's sisters tell me that my wound, the hole in my hand, entitles him to some payment. But not for the awful injuries that left him scarred.

In waking life, all the time I was with Will, he was mad about the ugly divorce he'd been through. As the dream put it, he couldn't get any settlement. "Settlement" is a perfect word here, because it is both *benefit* and *ease*. It is the benefit and ease we get from facing our pain. This always frustrated me, that he wouldn't work with it, just complain. But the dream says that he *couldn't*, because some sly city officials thwarted his attempts. Bureaucrats, I mused. Hm. Red tape.

Because of this dream, I see his inability to "do his work" in a new way. He was powerless somehow. My wound allowed him a little settlement, because of the rich conversations about my sorrow that we had after we broke up, but he could not lean into his own deep pain about the divorce. The dream shows this blockage but forgives it. The bureaucrats are part of his story; they're somewhere in him, but they are not the whole of him. He may have been trying to get some settlement, some freedom, but kept tripping over snarls of his own red tape.

He's not the only one with red tape, though. Look at my bandage in the dream!

I look up "red tape" and discover that the red tape used to tie up legal documents is not shiny and smooth like electrical tape; it's dark red and stringy. It looks *exactly* like the bloody adhesive tape on my hand.

The dream's final message is to take that saturated bandage off and go into town.

Here we see the final and deepest magic of this dream.

"Be concentrated and leonine/in the hunt for your true nourishment," says Rumi. Well, that was me. And on the long hunt for my true nourishment, I was something like that snow lion. The dream drives me up into the high country, where I can see an overview of my life adventure. I get to see the full glory, the full brushstroke beauty of my hunting energy. And then I see it die.

But what happens at that moment is the great gift of this dream. The dying cat pierces a hole in my hand, the side of my right hand, all the way through the car door.

I rub the place on my hand. Since I write longhand, that is the spot that brushes against the paper.

It's ink, I realize. Jesus. I shiver. The blood coming out of the hole in my hand is *ink*.

As I work on this dream, I keep being niggled by a memory of the Irish tale about the salmon of wisdom. I first heard this story when I was a little girl, maybe four years old.

> *An old salmon lived on the nuts of the nine hazel trees of wisdom that surrounded his pool, and thus became the wisest creature in the world. The poet Finegas spent seven long years trying to catch him. When he finally caught the fish, he handed it to his servant, Finn, to cook, with a stern warning not to eat any of it. While it was cooking over the fire, Finn burned his thumb on a drop of hot fat from the fish, and stuck his thumb in his mouth. And suddenly he knew everything—the speech of birds, the purpose of grief, the movement of a distant army. Sadly, Finegas gave him the rest of the salmon to eat, since the wisdom had already passed into him. All Finn's life, he could access this well of knowledge just by putting his thumb in his mouth.*

This story has never let go of me. The hazelnut trees, the pool, the boy who cooks the fish for his teacher and accidentally gets the power that his teacher has been seeking for so long. The sizzle of the hot fat, the smoke of the fire, the cold shadowy water, the overhanging nut trees, the tricky salmon, the grove in the faraway past, the boy turning the fish over and over on the spit over the fire.

I know now why this tale kept haunting me as I worked on the dream: It's a story of a passing on of power from an animal through a single wound on the hand. A burn. A hole.

The bright, sharp final message of my dream is as clear as a heartbeat.

"Pull off that red tape. Let your blood—your pain—your life-force—your ink!—flow, by god. "Things live fully only in departure," Rilke says. Let the snow lion's death be the beginning, not the end. Something happened when your hand was pierced? Maybe it's as deep and ancient as what happened to Finn when his thumb was burned. Come on, honey. Write the damn book. Go to town."

HAWK-EYE — *Dream*

March 14, 2020
66 years old

I'm standing in a park in England with a family who have invited me to join them on their journey. A red-tailed hawk is sitting on a branch of a nearby fir tree. I reach over and put my hand inside the hawk, between the body and the feathered skin. I hold it up above my head and it becomes a round, rippling sail of feathers, with the strong bony light quality of a wing, but circular, about three feet across. It's so alive. The red-brown feathers shiver in the wind.

In the center of this "wing" is a hole, a couple of inches across, and inside the hole is a strange, indescribable black strand, which is the bird's intelligence or mind. It's an astonishing feeling, holding this bird from the inside, feeling the life of it. Eventually I bring it down and set it back into the tree, and slowly, slowly withdraw my hand. It returns to its familiar hawk shape.

I say to the young man of the family, "That is possibly one of the coolest things that has occurred in my entire life."

He says we should celebrate and goes to get some champagne.

HAWK-EYE — *Reflection*

It is early March, with the smell of daphne and wet wood, rain rippling on the window. I shake my head, feeling again the weird miracle of putting my hand inside the hawk and lifting it into the sky.

A week after that dream, I suddenly got iritis, a painful inflammation of the iris in my right eye. (This is the illness I thought I had after looking into the bright light in the *Jeremy's Circus* dream.) I last had it twenty years ago, during the hard time with Jack. I heal it with a few steroid drops, but as with any odd physical symptom, I wonder about it, try to read it symbolically.

"If this were a dream . . ."? I write about iritis in my journal as rain spatters the glass.

Bang! It comes clear.

The rippling, circular, feathered sail that the hawk turns into when I put my hand inside it—that round wing with a hole in the center, through which the bird's intelligence can be glimpsed—is an *iris*. The hawk becomes an eye, when I hold it up. Hawk-eye!

HAWKEYE

We have been traveling hand in wing.

We are far from what you think, and so, dear heart, are you.

But in some sweet way, there is no *you*; there never was. Life shines through you, with you, not from you. We shine through you, and you through us.

We are more of a river than a boat, but we are a boat too. We are all of it. Not a breath or glacier or frog left out.

All my life, I've been on the lookout for magic. For the Wildwood, for Faery, for the world alive and miraculous, inhabited by countless beings in every rock and waterfall. And though it remains by nature elusive, I've found it, or it's found me.

Deep childhood has given me the purest taste of this extra-alive world, though that experience is still mostly a mystery. It comes, ushered in by a cold, about every two years. It tends to last two weeks (unless I'm in a Quaker community, when it lasts longer). I write about it every time. But I don't know what it is. The word *childhood* is probably a clue. It could be a body memory of my condition when I was four years old, playing in the New Hampshire woods among the pink ladyslippers and tiny-footed salamanders. I'm pretty sure I was more alive then, more animal-awake. But I wouldn't be surprised if it is a memory of somewhere else. I may have come, "trailing clouds of glory," from a place with wilder, cleaner air. Whatever it is, it is the sweetest, oddest thing.

But not the only thing. My trail has been studded with shards of the marvelous. The cold starry smell of Argenta Creek, the fire of standing on the tip of Mount Thielsen, the thrill of steering a tall ship through the night sea. The books I've read and been changed by—all those voices that have enlarged me beyond counting. The pleasures of learning: not only how to pluck a chicken and work my phone, but how to question my thoughts. How to speak up instead of shutting down. How to sit still.

How to be wrong! How to be smacked down and recover! My sexual misbehavior and infertility led me down a winding path to China, to the best daughters in the world. Losing my sisters helped me to face my own death and to sing at the bedsides of people who are dying. My gripping sorrow about Will gave me the great *Bark Europa* adventure and broke open a long-closed door. I've spent so much time trying not to make mistakes, but I see now that my griefs and failures were some of my most important work. They shaded me in, softened me up, made me better.

Dreams were key allies in this adventure, of course. They took me out among the stars, tucked my hand inside a hawk, flew me to Deep Alaska. They gave me insight, courage, and direct instructions. They weren't only rich experiences in themselves and wise teachers but a royal road to authentic conversations. I ask people to tell me their dreams because it is one way to find out what is really on their minds. The best of these conversations lead us into new territory. New territory! The surprise of uncovering what we didn't know! It's better than food.

None of this magic-hunting would have been possible without my fellow travelers. The dear friends who have responded to my cancer diagnosis with pizza and firewood and flowers, notes and prayers and invitations to use their beach cabin. Steve, with his honesty and sass. My dead but still-somehow-nearby relatives. I've become blindingly aware that I live in an old-growth forest of friends and family, a springy web of kinship.

When I set out long ago in search of the numinous—the Wildwood, the world beyond the world, whatever you like to call it—I was longing for a sense of depth and majesty, of wonder and meaning. The zillion ways in which that longing has been answered have been like brown, speckled feathers slowly filling out my wings. I expect, when the time comes to fly, that I will just ride right on out onto the wind.

HAWKEYE

We think your wings are grand.

Appendix I: THE BIG MESSAGES

All dreams have layers of meaning. Often they present an immediate and useful gift, and at the same time offer signposts and guidance for the long haul, the life journey. *Small Wild Book*, for instance, gave me a clear bookbinding assignment—but it also had a quality of cheering me on, encouraging my creativity. Many of the dreams in this book drew their force from the overlapping energy of one or more of these deeper messages. Here are the messages I heard, and the dreams I heard them from.

CREATE. WRITE. USE YOUR LIFE FORCE TO MAKE THINGS.
  Frogs and Thunderstorm
  Orange Tree
  Magical Tools
  Small Wild Book
  Apollo's World
  I'm the Cauldron
  Barbara Is Jealous of My Pretty Coat
  The Scarred Man and the Snow Lion

YOU ARE BEING HELPED.
  The Voice (telling me about deep childhood)
  God as a Cow
  Tap Dancing Mouse
  Predator
  Give Up, It's All Being Taken Care Of
  Magical Tools
  The New Law
  Why Am I Going through All This?
  Ambuchi
  Hawk-eye
  Preparing for the Big One

ASK BIG. SHOW UP. DON'T BE SO PASSIVE.
ACT ON YOUR OWN BEHALF.
  Ask for Horses
  God as a Cow
  Witta
  Choosing Clothes for the End of the World
  Drowning Car

TIME IS NON-LINEAR.
  Moon Man
  Stars and Drop of Water
  Cat-Baby
  Faun's Garden
  Barge to Quimby Bay
  The Pyre
  Preparing for the Big One

BEING WRONG CAN BE JOYFUL, OR LEAD TO JOY.
  Isn't the Mind Amazing?
  Magical Tools
  Apollo's World

DO THE HARD THING. THROW YOURSELF IN.
INCREASE YOUR NEED.
  Weather Underground
  Isn't the Mind Amazing?
  Magical Tools
  The Pyre

MAGIC IS AFOOT.
  Deep Alaska
  Weather Underground
  Magical Tools
  Ask for Horses
  Isn't the Mind Amazing?

Apollo's World
Stars and Drop of Water
Jeremy's Circus
Baker in the Woods
Faraway Planet
The Cauldron
The Pyre
Hawk-eye

TO FACE OUR CURRENT CRISIS, WE NEED TO SEE
THAT EVERYTHING IS IN PLAY.
   Witta
   Jeremy's Circus
   Faraway Planet

LET GO, ALREADY.
   The New Law
   Give Up
   Rusty Car

STOP. STAND STILL. WAIT. SLOW DOWN. REST.
   Moon Man
   Magical Tools
   How You Make Change in the World
   Knights Errant
   Give Up

THE EARTH IS SACRED, ALIVE AND AWAKE.
WE ARE ANIMALS; WE BELONG.
   Deep Alaska
   Stars and Drop of Water
   Cell in the Great Being
   Pawprints in the Land
   Hawk-eye

DEATH IS SAFE. IT IS A THRESHOLD TO SOMETHING ELSE.
Four Dreams in Pari
Choosing Clothes for the End of the World
Drowning Car

YOU ARE FORGIVEN. ALL IS WELL.
God as a Cow
Isn't the Mind Amazing?
Drowning Car
Ambuchi
The Scarred Man and the Snow Lion

Summary—THE BIG MESSAGES

Create. Write. Use your life force to make things.
You are being helped.
Ask big. Show up. Don't be so passive. Act on your own
    behalf.
Time is non-linear.
Being wrong can be joyful, or lead to joy.
Do the hard thing. Throw yourself in. Increase your need.
Magic is afoot.
To face our current crisis, we need to see that everything is
    in play.
Let go, already.
Stop. Stand still. Wait. Slow down. Rest.
The Earth is alive and awake. We are animals; we belong.
Death is safe. It is a threshold to something else.
You are forgiven. All is well.

Appendix II: PROMPTS FOR DREAMWORK

Having trouble remembering your dreams? Keep a notebook by your bed and record even the smallest scrap you recall. Dreams generally start to appear as soon as they realize you are paying attention. Once you've written a dream down, given it a title, taken note of the feelings in it, here are some ways to play with it:

GET CURIOUS
Dreams never come to tell you what you already know, so lean into the unfinished quality of your dream. Poke around. Look things up. Be a detective of your own mind. Listen for puns and wordplay. Pay close attention to the emotions; the feelings are key. Try imagining that every part of the dream is some part of you. Learn to love the click, the body shift of "aha!" Notice synchronistic events in your waking life that might relate to your dream—bodily symptoms, unusual happenings. Keep wondering about the images that puzzle you. Don't be dogmatic; there's no "one size fits all" interpretation. Your dream is your dream. Only you know what it means. A dream may continue to reveal itself for a long time.

SHARE YOUR DREAM WITH OTHER PEOPLE
Tell it aloud to a friend. Ponder it together. Let them project their own meaning onto it, using the "If it were my dream . . ." format. Take a class! There are great online classes on, for instance, lucid dreaming, dream journal as art, Focusing in dreams. Find people to regularly share dreams with: join an online dream group or start one in your living room.

MAKE SOMETHING OF IT
Draw all or part of the dream. Storyboard it, like a movie. Make a collage. Sculpt, dance, sing it. Give special attention to the point of most intensity. Write out the dream, using only feeling words (sad, relieved, mystified . . .). Turn the dream into

a poem. Use it as a springboard for a novel or a play. Let your dream motivate you to act on your own behalf and on behalf of the planet.

Dreams are seeds, packed with energy and potential. Plant them in your waking life.

Tina Tau is the author of four books of poetry, including *The Golden Tree*. She is a bookbinder, teacher, dreamworker, mother, and artist, and has had more than her share of adventures. She lives in Portland, Oregon.